CREATIVE BIBLE LEARNING

Science & Cooking

Karyn Henley

STANDARD
PUBLISHING
Cincinnati, Ohio

Cover design by B-LIN
Inside illustrations by Rusty Fletcher
Design and typography by Sherry F. Willbrand
Project editor, Ruth Frederick

Published by The Standard Publishing Company, Cincinnati, Ohio
A division of Standex International Corporation

© 1997 Karyn Henley

04 03 02 01 00 99 98 97   5 4 3 2 1

Library of Congress Cataloging-in-Publication Data
Henley, Karyn.
   Creative Bible learning/by Karyn Henley.
   p. cm.
   Includes index.
   Contents: [1] Arts & crafts — [3] Science & cooking — [3] Storytelling.
   ISBN 0-7847-0698-0 (v. 1). — ISBN 0-7847-0699-9 (v. 2). —
ISBN 0-7847-0697-2 (v. 3)
   1. Christian education of children. 2. Christian education—
Activity programs. 3. Bible crafts. I. Title.
   BV1475.2.H464   1997
   268'.432—dc21   97-6393
                                                                CIP

Science & Cooking

• Introduction •

Young children learn best by doing. The more senses they use, the better they will learn. They love not only to listen, but also to see, touch, smell, and taste. This book is a collection of activities that will make use of all the child's senses. He will learn about interesting science facts that God built in to our world long ago. But more than that, he will learn Bible stories and principles as he works and plays. The child will be able to have fun with cooking activities, and at the same time be led to Bible truths.

You can use this book in two ways. If you have a Bible story for which you need an extra activity, turn to the index. Find that story listed in the index and read there a listing of the science (**S**) and cooking (**C**) activities which would be appropriate to use with that story. Or if you choose one of the science or cooking activities to do with children, you can link it to a Bible story by using one of the Bible stories suggested at the end of the activity.

Here are some helpful hints to keep in mind as you use this book.
• Find out if any of the children have allergies, so you can choose appropriate cooking activities.
• Remember to make sure that everyone's hands are washed before any cooking activity.
• Keep safety considerations in mind. Make sure children stay well away from hot surfaces and sharp knives.
• When spreading butter, peanut butter, or other toppings, a good substitute for plastic knives is craft sticks or clean Popsicle sticks.
• Let hot foods cool before eating them. They may be eaten warm, but not hot.
• Consider the time a cooking activity will take. You may want to schedule it toward the beginning of class time so it has time to cook, or so there's time for it to cool before you eat it. You can do another activity while you are waiting.

There's an old saying that goes, "What I hear, I forget. What I see, I remember. "What I do, I know." So do a lot, learn a lot, and have fun!

Contents

Science

Flashlight Lantern	8
Seed Starters	9
Shadow Tracings	10
Earthworms	11
Hand Friction	12
Dandelion Seeds	13
Cinnamon Potpourri	14
Liquid Soap	15
Air: What You Can't See	16
Feather Pushing	17
Rock Scratching	18
Rock Salt	19
Grape Jelly Bird Feeder	20
Insects	21
Weather Wheel	22
Texture Walk	23
Smelling Chart	24
Eyes	25
Taste the Difference	26
Sound Matching	27
Face Sculpture	28
My Body	29
A Good Roof	30
What's It Made Of?	31
Where Do They Go?	32
Treasure Hunt	33
Erosion	34
Light on the Path	35
Peaceful Water	36
Tornado in a Bottle	37
Volcano	38
Roots	39
Leaves	40
Grain	41
Seed Matching	42
Light to See	43
Pets	44
Which Season?	45
Water Pouring	46
Water Magnifier	47
Night Sparkles	48
Heavy and Light	49
Natural Laws	50
Block Bed	51
Will It Last?	52
Animals Talk and Walk	53
Sound Waves	54
Music Maker	55
Balance Beam	56
Building Higher	57
Oil and Water	58
Seasonal Smells	59
Falling	60
Boiled Egg	61
Magnets	62
Bubble Rainbow	63
Rainbow Crayons	64
Mixing Colors	65
Translucent or Transparent	66
Pop the Corn	67
Pulling	68
Sink or Float	69
Paper Jail	70
Push a Box	71
Fire Safety	72
Measuring	73
Big and Little Clothes	74

Cooking

Hot Chocolate Mix	76
Chicken Noodle Soup	77
Fruity Cream Cheese Sandwiches	78

Contents

English Muffin Animals	79	
Rainbow Cake	80	
Treasure Salad	81	
Arrow Cheese Toast	82	
Kiss Cookies	83	
Ham Rolls	84	
Chocolate Cherry Bird Nests	85	
Apple Honey Nutters	86	
Sweet Potatoes With Cinnamon	87	
Moon Cookies	88	
Apple Wheel Pancakes	89	
Cheese Logs	90	
Corn Cake Lions	91	
Fruit Pies	92	
Happy Face Cookies	93	
Barley Soup	94	
Biscuit Sheep	95	
Giant Cookie	96	
Honey Pops	97	
Honey Crunch Bananas	98	
Cinnamon Angels	99	
Cooperation Cookies	100	
Heavenly Fruit Snack	101	
Egg Salad Sandwich	102	
Color Cookies	103	
Peanut Butter	104	
Silver Dollar Pancakes	105	
Tuna Salad	106	
Pita Pocket Message	107	
Cracker Fish in Soup	108	
Peanut Butter Delight	109	
Apricot Tea	110	
English Muffin Pizza	111	
Candlesticks	112	
Floating Cloud	113	
Pine-Orange Whip	114	
Sunshine Muffins	115	

Toasty Peanut Sticks	116	
Crunchy Chewies	117	
Treasure Cookies	118	
Edible Map	119	
Fish Dinner	120	
Mangers	121	
Noodle Nibbles	122	
Fruit Harvest Pizza	123	
Peach Sherbet	124	
Honey Cookies	125	
Hot Cider	126	
Health Muffins	127	
Double Thumbprint Cookies	128	
Rapid Rise Rolls	129	
Pigs in a Blanket	130	
Breadstick People	131	
Cinnamon Stars	132	
Apple Cinnamon Muffins	133	
Banana Muffins	134	
Mini Icees	135	
Dyed Eggs	136	
Cheese Fry Campfires	137	
Gingerbread People	138	
Cinnamon Toast	139	
Scroll Rolls	140	
Berry Bush Pies	141	
Fruit Punch	142	
Cloud Gelatin	143	
Fruit Yogurt Sundaes	144	
Bloomin' Apple	145	
Rainbow Sandwiches	146	
Flower Cookies	147	
Lemonade	148	
Cinnamon Cookies	149	
Storm Soup	150	
Index	151	

Science

Flashlight Lantern

Materials

one clean half-gallon plastic milk jug for each child
scissors for teacher use
one flashlight with batteries for each child
a variety of stickers

Guide Each Child To

1. Help the teacher cut off the top portion of the milk jug above the handle as shown.
2. Decorate the sides of the jug with stickers.
3. Set a flashlight in the jug with the light on, pointing down.
4. Hold the lantern by the jug handle to carry it, or hang it by the handle.

Talk About

- Where does light come from?
- Who made light? When?
- When do you need light most? What kinds of lights do you have where you live?
- What kind of light was in our story? What happened?

Suggested Bible Stories

Creation of Light and Color
God's Promise to Abraham
Jacob's Dream
Gideon
Samuel Hears God
David Spares Saul's Life at Night
Solomon's Dream
Elisha's Room on the Roof
Jesus Is Born
Paul to Damascus
Peter Escapes From Prison

1.

2.

3.

4.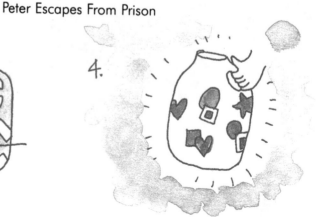

Seed Starters

Materials
egg shell halves, empty and clean
potting soil
seeds (marigold or radish)
plastic spoons
old newspapers
water

Guide Each Child To
1. Help spread old newspapers over the work surface.
2. Spoon potting soil into an eggshell half.
3. Plant a small seed in the potting soil.
4. Put a spoonful of water in the soil to moisten it. (When the seed sprouts, the child can plant it in the ground, cracking the shell before setting it in.)

Talk About
- What will grow from this seed?
- What does a seed need in order to grow?
- Did you ever have a garden? What did you grow?
- What grew in our story?

Suggested Bible Stories
Creation of Plants
Garden of Eden
Ruth
The Sower and the Seeds
The Wheat and the Weeds

Shadow Tracings

Materials

several pieces of plain white paper for each child
crayons
a sunny room or outdoor area
stapler

Guide Each Child To

1. Get a piece of paper and one crayon.
2. Find an interesting shadow, and put the paper on the edge of the shadow.
3. Trace around the shadow on the paper.
4. Make more shadow tracings on other sheets of paper.
5. Stack his shadow tracings together and staple them on the left side to make a booklet.

Talk About

• Who put the sun in the sky?
• What does the sun do?
• What is a shadow? How can you make a shadow? Do shadows always stay the same size?
• Tell about the sun, shade, or shadow in our story. What happened?

Suggested Bible Stories

Creation of Sun, Moon, and Stars
The Sun Stands Still
King Hezekiah Gets Well
Jonah

Earthworms

Materials
large jar
moist dirt in a container with a lid with holes in it
earthworms in the moist dirt
plastic spoons
lettuce, chopped into fine bits
bits of grass
play dough (ready-made or homemade by mixing 3
    parts flour, 1 part salt, and 1 part water)

Prepare Ahead of Time
Gather the dirt and earthworms.

Guide Each Child To
1. Help spoon the dirt into the jar.
2. Put earthworms into the jar with the dirt.
3. Sprinkle bits of grass and finely chopped lettuce
on top of the dirt.
4. Observe the earthworms.
5. Make "worms" out of play dough.

Talk About
• Did you ever find worms in dirt? How did you find them? What did they do?
• Who made worms? What other kinds of animals did God make?
• What's your favorite animal?
• Sometimes fishermen put worms on a fish hook and use them to catch fish. The fish comes up to eat the worm and bites the hook. Then the fisherman pulls the fish out of the water! Did you ever go fishing? What was it like?
• Who went fishing in our story? What happened?

Suggested Bible Stories
Creation of Animals
Noah
Jesus Chooses Twelve Friends (the fishermen)
The Great Catch of Fish
Tax Money in a Fish
Jesus Makes Breakfast for His Friends

Hand Friction

Materials
hand lotion

Guide Each Child To
1. Rub her hands on carpet or rough fabric.
2. Rub her hands on a smooth floor or table top. Compare how each feels.
3. Rub her hands together. Feel them getting warm.
4. Put lotion on her palms and her rub hands together again to feel the difference.

Talk About
- Who made your hands?
- Do your hands ever get cold? How do you get them warm again?
- When you rub your hands on something rough, you feel friction. Friction makes you have to push your hand harder to rub. But on the smooth floor there's not as much friction. It's easier to rub. When you put lotion on your hands, was it easier to rub or harder?
- What are some helpful things you can do with your hands?
- What happened to the hands in our story?

Suggested Bible Stories
Creation of People
Burning Bush
Writing on the Wall
The Man's Withered Hand

Dandelion Seeds

Materials

one piece of colored construction paper for each
   child
colored glue
dandelions that have gone to seed

Guide Each Child To

1. Spread colored glue in a design on his paper.
2. Blow dandelion seeds onto the glue.

Talk About

• What grows from a bean seed? What grows
from a carrot seed? What grows from an
apple seed? What grows from a dandelion
seed?

• Dandelion seeds travel. How do they get
from one place to another? How do other
seeds get from place to place?

• Did you ever plant a seed? Where? What
happened?

• What does a seed need in order to grow?

• Who made seeds?

• What plants grew in our story?

Suggested Bible Stories

Creation of Plants
Pharaoh's Dreams
Ruth
Jonah
Birds and Flowers (Sermon on the Mount)
The Sower and the Seeds
The Triumphal Entry

Cinnamon Potpourri

Materials
whole stick cinnamon
whole cloves
dried orange peels
ground cinnamon
ground cloves
mixing bowl
one plastic sandwich bag for each child
6 inches of narrow ribbon for each child
3-by-5-inch index cards
hole punch
pen

Prepare Ahead of Time
Cut the index cards in half. Print on each half card: "Cover with water and simmer. Add more water as needed."

Guide Each Child To
1. Break the cinnamon sticks and orange peel into smaller pieces.
2. Mix together cinnamon sticks, orange peel, cloves (whole and ground), and ground cinnamon.
3. Put some of this mixture into her bag.
4. Fold one of the index card halves so the writing is on the inside.
5. Punch a hole in the top left side of her folded card.
6. Thread the ribbon through the hole and then help the teacher tie the ribbon around the top of the potpourri bag.
7. Take the potpourri home and give it as a gift.

Talk About
• God wants us to be cheerful givers. What does that mean?
• Why would God want us to be cheerful givers?
• How do you feel when someone gives you something nice?
• How do other people feel when you give them something nice?
• Who was a giver in our story? What happened?

Suggested Bible Stories
Creation of Plants
Isaac Gets a Wife
Joseph's Colorful Coat
Samuel's New Coats
David and Jonathan
Queen of Sheba
The Wise Men
The Widow's Mite

Liquid Soap

Materials (for every six containers of soap)
one 3½-ounce bar of moisturizing soap
3 cups of water
one plastic travel container (5 ounces or smaller)
   for each child
cheese grater
large microwaveable bowl
microwave oven
measuring cup
mixing spoon

Guide Each Child To

1. Help grate the soap into the bowl.
2. Add 3 cups of water to the grated soap.
3. Microwave the soap and water mixture on high for 5 to 6 minutes.
4. Stir well and let the mixture cool.
5. Pour some of the soap into a travel container for himself.

Talk About

• At first, the soap was a solid. It couldn't pour out like water. After we added water and let it get mixed in, it was a liquid. It could pour out.
• What do we use soap for?
• How do you help at home? How do you help in class?
• Who was a helper in our story? What happened?

Suggested Bible Stories

Pharaoh's Dream (Joseph cleans up to see him)
Baby Moses (Miriam watches and helps)
Ruth
Naaman (the servant girl helps)
Mary and Martha
Dorcas

Air: What You Can't See

Materials

clean, empty plastic soft drink bottle
sink or bowl of water large enough to submerge the
drink bottle

Guide Each Child To

1. Examine the soft drink bottle and tell if he thinks
there's anything in it. (There is something in it.)
2. Take a turn submerging the bottle and watching
what's inside it (air) come out.

Talk About

• What was inside the bottle? How do you
know?
• Can you see air? How do you know it's
there?
• Can you see God? How do you know he's
there?
• What do we call it when air is blowing on
us and it blows our hair and it blows the
leaves?
• Who felt the wind in our story? What
happened?

Suggested Bible Stories

Crossing the Red Sea
Elijah Goes Up to Heaven
Jesus Stills the Storm
Jesus Walks on Water
Paul's Shipwreck

Feather Pushing

Materials
plastic squeeze bottles
feathers

Guide Each Child To
1. Place a feather on the table or floor.
2. Try moving the feather by using the bottle to squeeze air at it.
3. Try blowing the feather.
4. Try moving other things with the air from a squeeze bottle (hair, leaves, sand, and so on).

Talk About
• Air can move a feather. What else can air move? Air is strong. Air has power. But who's the strongest of all?
• What else is powerful and strong? Electricity (plug in a lamp), batteries (put them in a flashlight or radio), and our muscles. Who is the strongest and most powerful of all?
• How did God show his power in our story?

Suggested Bible Stories
Crossing the Red Sea
Jericho's Walls Fall Down
The Sun Stands Still
Elijah on Mt. Carmel
Elijah Goes Up to Heaven
Daniel and the Lions
Lame Man at the Pool
Jairus's Daughter
Lazarus
The Resurrection
Paul and Silas in Prison

Rock Scratching

Materials

large and small rocks
charcoal
white paper
wet wipes
chalk
black paper

Guide Each Child To

1. Choose two rocks—a large one and a small one. Try rubbing them together to see if any dust rubs off.
2. Scratch the rocks on each other to see if they make a mark. Find out if one seems harder than the other.
3. Use charcoal to draw a picture on white paper. Clean his hands off with wet wipes.
4. Use chalk to draw a picture on black paper.

Talk About

• Where can you find rocks?
• What do people do with rocks?
• Do you have any rocks where you live?
• What happened with the rock(s) in our story?

Suggested Bible Stories

Water From a Rock
David and Goliath
Elijah on Mt. Carmel
Jesus Is Tempted
The Resurrection (stone rolled away)

Rock Salt

Materials
rock salt
table salt
magnifying glass
microscope (optional)
paper plates

Guide Each Child To
1. Put some table salt and some rock salt on a plate.
2. Examine the salt. Look at it. Feel it. Look at it under a magnifying glass and microscope, if possible. See that it is a rock.

Talk About
• Salt is a kind of rock that we eat. When do you eat salt?
• What does the salt look like?
• Who made your eyes so you can see and learn?
• What did the person in our story see? What happened?

Suggested Bible Stories
Servant Sees God's Army
Jesus Heals a Blind Man With Mud
Blind Bartimaeus
Paul to Damascus

Grape Jelly Bird Feeder

Materials
one orange half for each child
one plastic spoon for each child
sturdy toothpicks
yarn
grape jelly
bird seed
30 inches of yarn or string for each child

Guide Each Child To
1. Eat her orange half and then scoop out the rest of the insides.
2. Punch one hole in each side of the orange rind with a toothpick. Wiggle the toothpick around in the holes to make the holes bigger.
3. Thread yarn through the holes so the orange half will hang. Tie the yarn to each side as shown.
4. Put bird seed in the orange half.
5. Scoop grape jelly on top.

Talk About
• In winter, grape jelly is a good energy food for birds. Why would birds need energy in the wintertime?
• What else do birds eat?
• Do you have pets at home? What do they eat?
• What happened with the bird(s) in our story?

Suggested Bible Stories
Creation of Animals
Noah
Ravens Feed Elijah
Jesus Is Baptized
Birds and Flowers (Sermon on the Mount)

1.
2.
3.
4. & 5.

Insects

Materials
plastic jars with small holes in the lids or netting
  over the openings secured with rubber bands
a variety of live insects, one in each jar, with a few
  twigs, leaves, and some grass
magnifying glass

Variation: Allow the children to hunt and catch insects to put into the jars.

Variation: Make a dead insect collection by pinning dead insects to a piece of corrugated cardboard with straight pins. You can often find dead insects in windowsills and on the front grills of cars.

Guide Each Child To
1. Hunt and catch insects outdoors if possible, or arrange the jars of insects on a table.
2. Observe the insects. Notice the wings and antennae. Count the body parts and legs.
3. After observing the live insects, set them free outside.

Talk About
- Who made animals?
- How are insects different from other animals?
- One insect makes honey. What is it?
- One insect used to be a caterpillar. What is it?
- Why is it important to set live insects free after watching them for awhile?
- What insects were in our story?

Suggested Bible Stories
Creation of Animals
Noah
The Plagues in Egypt (flies, locusts, and gnats)
John the Baptist (locusts)

Weather Wheel

Materials
one small piece of poster board for each child
paper plates
blunt scissors
paper fasteners (brads)
crayons

Guide Each Child To
1. Put a paper plate in the center of his poster board and trace around it to make a circle.
2. Help the teacher draw one line across the circle from top to bottom and another one from side to side to make four sections.
3. Draw a sun in one section, rain in another, a cloud in another, and snow in another (or a tree bending in the wind, if it doesn't snow where you live).
4. Help the teacher cut off one-fourth of the paper plate.
5. Place the plate on top of the circle and attach it in the center with a paper fastener.
6. Turn the opening in the plate so that the current weather is showing.

Talk About
• Name some different kinds of weather.
• What would you wear in these kinds of weather?
• What's your favorite kind of weather?
• What kind of weather was in our story? What happened?

Suggested Bible Stories
Noah
The Plagues in Egypt
The Sun Stands Still
Elijah on Mt. Carmel (servant sees a cloud)
Jonah
Jesus Stills the Storm
Jesus Walks on Water
Paul's Shipwreck

1.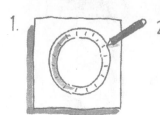
2.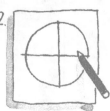
3.
4.
5.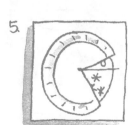

Texture Walk

Materials

a variety of materials to walk on (cotton balls, linoleum tiles, tightly woven and shaggy carpet samples, masking tape with the sticky side up, sandpaper, leaves, a piece of plywood, cardboard)

Guide Each Child To

1. Remove his shoes and socks.
2. Place his shoes and socks neatly at one side of the room, so they can be easily located at the end of the activity.
3. Walk over the textured material.

Talk About

• Texture is the way something feels when you touch it. Things can be soft or hard, rough or smooth, and so on. How does this cotton feel to your feet? Have you ever felt anything else like this before? Is it soft or hard?

• Who made textures? Who made our skin able to feel these textures?

• We walked over this path. In Bible times, most people walked when they traveled. Who traveled in our story? Where did they go?

Suggested Bible Stories

Abraham Travels
Isaac Gets a Wife
Joseph Is Taken to Egypt
Crossing the Red Sea
Israelites Wander in the Wilderness
Ruth
Queen of Sheba
Rebuilding Jerusalem's Walls (people return)
The Wise Men
Joseph, Mary, and Jesus Go to Egypt
Jesus Walks on Water
The Good Samaritan
The Triumphal Entry
Philip and the Man From Ethiopia

Smelling Chart

Materials

one piece of construction paper for each child
four small squares of felt for each child
vanilla extract
peppermint flavoring
perfume
cinnamon
glue
eye droppers

Guide Each Child To

1. Glue four felt squares onto construction paper.
2. With a dropper, add a few drops of a liquid scent to one square of felt. Repeat using the other two scents.
3. Rub cinnamon onto the remaining square.
4. Smell the scents, trying to identify each one.

Talk About

- How does this smell? What is it?
- Where might you smell it?
- Who made smells?
- Who made noses to smell with?
- What might you have smelled if you had been there when our story happened?

Suggested Bible Stories

Creation of People
Noah
Elijah on Mt. Carmel
Daniel Refuses the King's Food
Jonah
The Wise Men
The Great Catch of Fish
Jesus Feeds 5,000
Perfume on Jesus' Feet
The Lord's Supper
Jesus Makes Breakfast for His Friends

Eyes

Materials

one full-length mirror (or one small mirror for each child)

Prepare Ahead of Time

Turn the full-length mirror sideways so the children can sit in front of it.

Guide Each Child To

1. Sit in front of the mirror.
2. Watch his pupils to see how they dilate as the teacher turns the classroom lights off, and then on again.
3. Touch his eyebrows and eyelashes, wink and blink, and so on.

Talk About

• Your pupils are what you see through. They are like windows. The eyelashes and eyebrows keep dust and sweat out of your eyes. Your eyelids are your window shades. They close when you sleep and wink and blink. And when something is coming toward your eye very fast, they close to protect your eye.
• Why do we close our eyes to pray?
• Who made our eyes?
• How can a person who is blind tell about the world around him if he can't see?

Suggested Bible Stories

Creation of People
Samson
Jesus Heals a Blind Man With Mud
Blind Bartimaeus
Paul to Damascus

Taste the Difference

Materials

¼ cup salt in a bowl
¼ cup sugar in a bowl
oranges or grapefruit, peeled and sectioned
one square of unsweetened baking chocolate, unwrapped
one plain milk chocolate candy bar, unwrapped
paper towels

Guide Each Child To

1. Look at the bowls of salt and sugar and guess which is which without tasting them.
2. Dip an orange slice or grapefruit slice in one bowl of his choice. Taste it and tell whether it was salt or sugar.
3. Look at the two pieces of chocolate and tell which one looks like it will taste the best.
4. Break a small piece off of the one that looked the best. Try it to see how it tastes. Now try the other one to see how it tastes.

Talk About

• Was it hard or easy to tell the difference in the salt and sugar and the sweet and bitter chocolate by just looking? Did you make the right choice and get the taste you wanted?
• Sometimes it's hard to choose what's right. What if you are angry at someone? What choices can you make? Which is the right choice?
• What did the person in our story choose to do? Did they make the right choice or the wrong choice? What happened?

Suggested Bible Stories

Adam and Eve Eat the Fruit
Abraham and Lot
Twelve Spies
Ruth
David Spares Saul's Life at Night
Esther
The Fiery Furnace
Daniel and the Lions
Jonah
Jesus Is Tempted
Mary and Martha
Zacchaeus

Sound Matching

Materials

ten clean, empty soda cans
unpopped popcorn
dried beans
paper clips
uncooked rice
salt
tape

Prepare Ahead of Time

Put unpopped popcorn in two cans, dried beans in two cans, paper clips in two cans, rice in two cans, and salt in two cans. Securely tape over the opening of each can. Mix up the cans.

Guide Each Child To

1. Shake the cans.
2. Try to find the pairs that sound alike and set them side by side.
3. Use the cans to accompany worship and praise songs in class.

Talk About

• Which cans sound loud? Which sound soft? Which do you like best?
• What is a musical instrument? What are some instruments we can use to praise God?
• What is your favorite instrument?
• What would you like to praise God for now? Who praised God in our story?

Suggested Bible Stories

Crossing the Red Sea (Israelites praise God)
David Plays the Harp
Solomon Builds the Temple (the dedication)
Singers Lead Jehoshaphat's Army
Rebuilding Jerusalem's Walls (people praise God)
Angels Appear to the Shepherds
Anna and Simeon
The Triumphal Entry
Peter and John Heal the Lame Man
Paul and Silas in Prison
John Sees Heaven

Face Sculpture

Materials

one large sheet of aluminum foil for each child
one large piece of construction paper for each
   child
stapler

Guide Each Child To

1. Gently mold a sheet of foil around her face and
sculpt her features.
2. Carefully staple the edges of the foil sculpture to
the construction paper to make it easier to carry.

Talk About

• Who made you? Do you look like anyone
in your family? How are you different and
special?
• God made each part of your body to have
a special job. What job do your eyes do?
What job do your ears do?
• In our story, whose eyes couldn't see
(or mouth speak)? What happened?

Suggested Bible Stories

John the Baptist Is Born (Zechariah is unable to
   speak)
Jesus Heals a Blind Man With Mud
Blind Bartimaeus
Paul to Damascus

My Body

Materials
measuring tape
small, soft ball for indoor use

Guide Each Child To
1. Measure the distance he can jump from a standing position.
2. Measure the distance he can throw a ball.
3. Stand facing a wall, jump up and touch as high as he can. Measure the height. Feel his pulse while he is resting, run in place for thirty seconds, then feel his pulse again. Compare how his pulse felt after he ran with how it felt before he ran.

Talk About
• Who made your body? God made all parts to work together.
• When you get sick, does it change what you can do with your whole body?
• What are some things you can do when you are sick?
• Who was sick in our story? What happened?

Suggested Bible Stories
Naaman
King Hezekiah Gets Well
Peter's Mother-in-Law
Through the Roof
The Centurion's Sick Servant
The Man's Withered Hand
Woman Touches Jesus' Hem
Jairus's Daughter
Jesus Heals the Bent Woman
Ten Lepers
Lazarus
Peter and John Heal a Lame Man
Dorcas

A Good Roof

Materials

large cake pan
blocks
piece of cloth
tissue paper
napkin
water
8-by-8-inch square of wood
square of cotton batting
smaller metal pan
leaves and twigs
aluminum foil
Styrofoam plate
pitcher

Guide Each Child To

1. Help build a small block house without a roof in the cake pan.
2. Place the cloth over the house to make a roof.
3. Pour water over the cloth to see if it makes a good roof or not.
4. Repeat the process using the different materials suggested to find a good roof for the house.

Talk About

• If water goes through the roof, the material is porous. If it doesn't go through, the material is nonporous.
• Why couldn't you live outside all the time?
• A place that keeps us dry and warm and safe is called a shelter. The place where you live is a shelter for you. What do you like about the place where you live?
• What were the people in our story building? What happened?

Suggested Bible Stories

Noah
Tower of Babel
Building the Tabernacle
Jericho's Walls Fall Down
Solomon Builds the Temple
Elisha's Room on the Roof
Rebuilding Jerusalem's Walls
The Wise Man's House
Bigger Barns

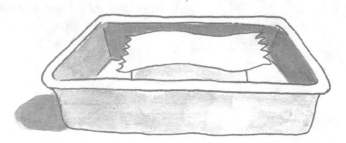

What's It Made Of?

Materials
messy room with toys that need to be picked up

Guide Each Child To
1. Watch as the teacher shows a toy made of wood.
2. When the teacher says "Go" help her classmates pick up all toys made of wood and put them in their proper places.
3. Watch as the teacher shows a toy made of plastic.
4. When the teacher says "Go," help her classmates pick up all toys made of plastic and put them in their proper places.
5. Watch as the teacher shows a piece of paper.
6. When the teacher says "Go," help her classmates pick up all the paper and put it in its proper place. (Continue in this way until all the toys have been picked up.)

Talk About
• How can you tell what something is made of? What does plastic feel like? What does wood feel like? What does paper feel like?
• What does it mean to *obey*? How did you obey in this game?
• Who obeyed in our story? What happened?

Suggested Bible Stories
The Ten Commandments
Samuel Hears God
A Widow's Oil Jars
Naaman
Daniel Refuses the King's Food
Jonah
The Great Catch of Fish
Two Sons and a Vineyard

Where Do They Go?

Materials
pictures of the land, sea, and sky
pictures of different animals that live on land, in
    water, and that fly in the sky
three large grocery bags
glue

Prepare Ahead of Time
Glue or draw a picture of the land on one bag, a
picture of the sea on another bag, and a picture of
the sky on the last bag.

Guide Each Child To
1. Help pass out animal pictures to everyone.
2. Take a turn putting his animal pictures in the
bag that has the picture of where the animals live
and move around.

Talk About
• Where does this animal live? Is there something special about the way he's made that lets you know where he lives? Who made this animal?
• Where do you live? Have you ever been in the water? Have you ever flown in the sky? Could you stay in either of these places?

Suggested Bible Stories
Creation of Sky, Sea, and Land
Creation of Animals
Noah
Balaam's Talking Donkey
Ravens Feed Elijah
Daniel and the Lions
The Great Catch of Fish
Birds and Flowers (Sermon on the Mount)
Tax Money in a Fish

Treasure Hunt

Materials
magnifying glasses
spoons or shovels
small paper sacks

Guide Each Child To
1. Choose a paper sack and spoon.
2. Go outdoors and dig in an area where there's dirt, if possible.
3. Gather rocks, leaves, or other "treasures," and place them in her sack.
4. Examine the treasures under a magnifying glass.

HINT: If you cannot dig, try to gather the treasures from above the ground and examine them.

Talk About
• What did the man in Jesus' story find? What did he do?
• What is like that treasure to us? What is God's kingdom? (Wherever God is king, that's where God's kingdom is. If God is king of your heart, you are in God's kingdom. God's kingdom is like a treasure.)

Suggested Bible Stories
Creation of Sky, Sea, and Land
Hidden Treasure

Erosion

Materials
container of sand
container of rocks
pitcher of water

Guide Each Child To
1. Take a turn pouring water over the sand and over the rocks.
2. Describe what happened to each as he poured water.

Talk About
• What would happen to your house if it were built on this sand?
• Has it ever rained hard where you live? What happened in the story?

Suggested Bible Stories
Noah
Jesus Stills the Storm
The Wise Man's House
Paul's Shipwreck

Light on the Path

Materials
8-to-12-inch footprints cut from construction paper or cardboard
masking tape

Prepare Ahead of Time
Tape footprints to the floor in any pattern that forms a path.

Guide Each Child To
1. Line up to follow the path with the lights turned off.
2. Try to slowly walk the path without seeing it.
3. See where he ended up when the lights are turned back on.

Talk About
• You must have light in order to see. The objects you see are bouncing, or reflecting, light to your eye. But when it is dark, they cannot bounce or reflect light to your eye. So you cannot see them.
• How does a person who is blind get around? Who was blind in our story? What happened?
• Where did the light come from in our story? What happened?

Suggested Bible Stories
Blindness:
Jesus Heals a Blind Man With Mud
Blind Bartimaeus
Paul to Damascus

Light:
Creation of Light and Color
God Leads Israel With a Pillar of Fire
The Sun Stands Still
Gideon
Let Your Light Shine
Paul to Damascus
John Sees Heaven

Peaceful Water

Materials
two transparent heat resistant glasses or jars
tea kettle
water
food coloring
stove or hot plate (or bring one thermos of
    steaming hot water and one thermos of cold
    water)

Guide Each Child To
1. Let the teacher boil the water.
2. Watch the teacher fill one glass with hot water
and the other glass with cold water.
3. Add a drop of food coloring to each glass.
4. Describe what she sees in the glasses. (The hot
water swirls faster. The cold water is more still.)

Talk About
• Which glass of water looks more peaceful?
Why?
• Did you ever feel inside like that glass of
hot water—boiling and swirling? What would
you call that feeling?
• Did you ever feel like the glass of cold
water—still and calm? What would you call
that feeling? Who gives us peace? Who felt
peace in our story?

Suggested Bible Stories
Abraham and Lot
David Plays the Harp (for Saul)
Angels Appear to the Shepherds ("peace on earth")
The Beatitudes (Sermon on the Mount)
Jesus Stills the Storm

hot   cold

Tornado in a Bottle

Materials
transparent soft drink bottle with a lid
water
salt
dishwashing liquid
measuring spoons
pictures of different kinds of weather

Guide Each Child To
1. Help fill the bottle about two-thirds full with water.
2. Add ¼ teaspoon salt if it's a small bottle and ½ teaspoon salt if it's a large bottle.
3. Add two drops of dishwashing liquid.
4. Close the bottle tightly.
5. Shake the bottle in a circular motion, from side to side.
6. Watch the swirling water tornado form in the center.
7. Look at and discuss the different pictures of weather.

Talk About
• How do you feel about storms? Where do you like to be in a storm?
• How did the people in the story feel about the storm? What happened?

Suggested Bible Stories
Noah
The Plagues in Egypt (hail)
Jonah
Jesus Stills the Storm
Jesus Walks on Water
Paul's Shipwreck

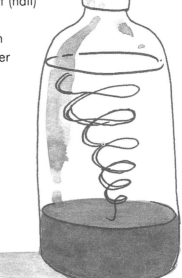

Volcano

Materials
aluminum foil
one short paper cup
¼ cup baking soda
vinegar
tablespoon

Guide Each Child To
1. Help wrap foil around the paper cup so that the foil slopes outward like the sides of a hill.
2. Put the baking soda into the cup.
3. Pour vinegar over the soda, one tablespoon at a time.

vinegar

aluminum foil

cup

baking soda

Talk About
• Have you ever seen pictures of a real volcano? What was it like?
• A volcano brings trouble for people who live around it. What kind of trouble did the people in our story have? What happened?
• Who helps us and takes care of us in times of trouble?
• Tell about a time when there was trouble for you, but God helped you.

Suggested Bible Stories
Noah
Crossing the Red Sea
David and Goliath
Servant Sees God's Army
The Fiery Furnace
Daniel and the Lions
Jesus Stills the Storm
Jesus Walks on Water
The Resurrection (earthquake)
Paul and Silas in Prison
Paul's Shipwreck

Roots

Materials

two small plants, one well-rooted in a pot and one
    pulled up, roots exposed
piece of stiff cardboard, about 8 by 11 inches for
    each child
table or other smooth surface
watering can filled with water

Guide Each Child To

1. Notice what is different about the two plants.
One is in the ground and one is pulled out of the
ground.
2. Take a good look at the root system of the
uprooted plant.
3. Fan a piece of cardboard at both plants to see
what happens to each plant.
4. Water the plant that is in the pot.

Talk About

• Who made plants? What are the roots on a
plant for? Which plant will not blow away?
Which plant will get water?
• What happened when you made the wind
blow on the plants?
• What kind of plants were in our story?
What happened?

Suggested Bible Stories

Creation of Plants
Garden of Eden
Burning Bush
Aaron's Staff Blooms
Birds and Flowers (Sermon on the Mount)
The Triumphal Entry
Jesus in Gethsemane
The Resurrection (garden tomb)

Leaves

Materials
leaves of all sizes and shapes
magnifying glass
two celery stalks with leaves
tall glass
water
red food coloring
one piece of plain white paper for each child
crayons

Prepare Ahead of Time
Put food coloring in a glass of water. Place one celery stalk in the colored water. Let it sit for several hours.

Guide Each Child To
1. Examine the leaves with and without the magnifying glass. Notice the differences and similarities.
2. Examine the plain celery stalk, noticing the veins or "straws" through which the plant drinks its water.
3. Examine the celery stalk that has been in the colored water. Tell what she thinks happened.
4. Choose several leaves to place under her piece of paper.
5. Color over the paper with crayons to reveal the leaf patterns underneath.

Talk About
- Which leaves do you like best?
- How do the leaves get water?
- What kinds of plants were in our story? What happened?

Suggested Bible Stories
Creation of Plants
Garden of Eden
Burning Bush
Aaron's Staff Blooms
Birds and Flowers (Sermon on the Mount)
Jesus in Gethsemane
The Resurrection (garden tomb)

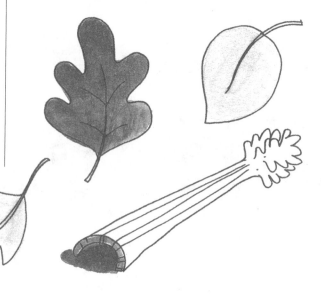

Grain

Materials
a variety of whole grains: wheat, corn, rice, oats,
   barley (available at health food stores)
unpopped popcorn
corn meal
corn chips
magnifying glass
metal, plastic, or wooden bowl
large, smooth rock

Guide Each Child To
1. Look at each kind of grain as you explain
about it.
2. Touch, smell, and examine the grain with the
magnifying glass.
3. Examine the unpopped corn, the corn meal,
and the corn chips to see how the grain can be
used in different forms.
4. Eat some corn chips.
5. Try to grind one of the grains of his choice with
the rock in the bowl.

Talk About
• How are these grains alike? How are they
different?
• What can people make out of grain?
• Who saw the grain in our story? What
happened?

Suggested Bible Stories
Joseph's Dreams
Pharaoh's Dreams
Joseph's Brothers Go to Egypt
Ruth
Bigger Barns
The Wheat and the Weeds

Seed Matching

Materials

one bell pepper, apple, grapefruit, lemon, squash
two peaches, plums, cherries
the end slice of a watermelon
one grape with seeds in it
fresh green beans
fresh green peas in pods
waxed paper

Prepare Ahead of Time

Cut the pepper, apple, grapefruit, lemon, squash, and grape in half. Take out a few seeds. Take the pits out of one peach, one plum, and one cherry. Take a few seeds out of the watermelon. Take a few bean and pea seeds out of the beans and peas.

Wash the seeds. Set out the fruit and vegetables on waxed paper with their cut sides down so the children can't see the seeds inside. Set the seeds out on another piece of waxed paper separate from the fruit and vegetables they came from.

Guide Each Child To

1. Look at the seeds.
2. Guess which food each seed came from.
3. Turn over each food as he guesses to see if he was correct.

Talk About

- Who made plants and seeds?
- What do we use plants for? Are all plants for eating?
- Name some plants we eat.
- What did the people in our story eat? What happened?
- What's your favorite food?

Suggested Bible Stories

Abraham and the Three Visitors
Birthright and Blessing
Joseph's Brothers Go to Egypt
Manna and Quail
Ruth
Ravens Feed Elijah
A Widow Shares With Elijah
Daniel Refuses the King's Food
Jesus Feeds 5,000
The Lord's Supper
Jesus Makes Breakfast for His Friends

Light to See

Materials
flashlight

Guide Each Child To
1. Sit in a darkened room and wait for the teacher to say, "Around and around I shine my beam. When it stops, what do you see?"
2. Look at the object that the teacher is shining the flashlight on, and tell what it is. Tell what it is used for.
3. Thank God for that object.

Talk About
• Who made our world? Who gives us all the good things we have? How can we thank God?
• Is there something you want to thank God for? How can we talk to God? Who said thank-you in our story? What happened?

Suggested Bible Stories
David Plays the Harp (Psalms)
Rebuilding Jerusalem's Walls
Jesus Feeds 5,000
Ten Lepers
Lazarus
The Lord's Supper
Road to Emmaus

Pets

Materials

gentle animal in a cage, box, or other container
food for the animal
any other simple animal care items for this animal
(for example, a brush for a cat)

Guide Each Child To

1. Look at the animal and describe it.
2. Notice the animal's feet, eyes, ears, and tail.
3. Watch how the animal moves around.
4. If the animal is very gentle, pet it and hold it.

Talk About

• Have you ever seen an animal like this before? Where?
• How would you take care of an animal like this?
• Who made animals? What other kinds of animals did God make?
• Do you have a pet at home? Tell about it.
• What was the animal in our story? What happened?

Suggested Bible Stories

Creation of Animals
Adam Names the Animals
Balaam's Talking Donkey
David, the Shepherd Boy
Ravens Feed Elijah
Daniel and the Lions
Jesus Is Born
Birds and Flowers (Sermon on the Mount)
Tax Money in a Fish
The Good Samaritan
The Lost Sheep
The Triumphal Entry

Which Season?

Materials
four large paper grocery bags
several magazine pictures of each season

Prepare Ahead of Time
Tape a picture of springtime on the front of one paper bag, a picture of summer on another, a picture of autumn on a third bag, and a picture of winter on the last bag. Set the empty bags in a row.

Guide Each Child To
1. Take a picture of one of the seasons. Place it in the bag with the picture of that same season.
2. Take turns with his classmates sorting the pictures into the bags according to seasons.

Talk About
• Who made the different seasons? Which is your favorite?
• What is spring like? Is God with you in the springtime?
• What is summer like? Is God with you in the summer?
• What is autumn like? Is God with you in the autumn?
• What is winter like? Is God with you in the winter?
• How did God show that he was with the person in our story? How does God show that he is with you?

Suggested Bible Stories
Noah
Ravens Feed Elijah
Singers Lead Jehoshaphat's Army
Daniel and the Lions
Jesus is Baptized
Jesus Stills the Storm
The Transfiguration
Peter Escapes From Prison
Paul and Silas in Prison
Paul on Malta

Water Pouring

Materials

large tub, water table, or sink
strainer
slotted spoon
funnels
one small and one large paper cup for each child
empty plastic milk jug

Guide Each Child To

1. Scoop water into her large paper cup and pour it all into her small cup. Notice what happens.
2. Scoop water with the strainer, the slotted spoon, and the funnels. Notice the difference in the rate that the water flows out of each.
3. Try to stand the empty milk jug up on top of the water.
4. Pour one cup of water into the milk jug to see if it will stand.
5. Keep pouring water into the jug until it finally stands upright in the water. Count how many cups it takes to make it stand.
6. Empty the milk jug. Guess how many cups of water it will take to fill it up.
7. Fill the milk jug with water, one cup at a time, counting how many cups it will take to see if her guess was correct.

Talk About

• What does water feel like? Have you ever gone swimming? What was it like?
• What do we call water that comes down from the sky?
• What is a storm like? Do you ever get scared in a storm?
• Who took care of the people in our story? Who takes care of you?

Suggested Bible Stories

Noah
The Plagues in Egypt
Jonah
John the Baptist
Jesus Is Baptized
Lame Man at the Pool
The Wise Man's House
The Woman at the Well
Jesus Stills the Storm
Jesus Walks on Water
Philip and the Man From Ethiopia
Peter and Cornelius
Lydia

Water Magnifier

Materials
waxed paper
eye dropper
bowl of water
newspaper
paper towels

Guide Each Child To
1. Spread a sheet of newspaper on the table in front of him.
2. Place a sheet of waxed paper on top of the newspaper.
3. With an eye dropper, get some water from the bowl and drip it into one small puddle on the waxed paper.
4. Gently slide the waxed paper over the newspaper and watch how the water magnifies the letters and pictures on the newspaper.

Talk About
• What happens to the letters and pictures on the newspaper? Why?
• Why do people use magnifying glasses?
• To magnify something is to make it big so everyone can see it. Sometimes we say we magnify the Lord. We tell how great he is so everyone can see how great he is.
• Sometimes we show how great God is by praising him. What is praise?
• Who praised God in our story? Why? How can we praise God?

Suggested Bible Stories
Crossing the Red Sea
David Plays the Harp
Singers Lead Jehoshaphat's Army
Angels Appear to the Shepherds
Anna and Simeon
Let Your Light Shine
The Triumphal Entry
The Resurrection
Peter and John Heal the Lame Man

Night Sparkles

Materials
wintergreen hard mints
dark room, closet, or a heavy blanket

Guide Each Child To
1. Hold a wintergreen mint.
2. Turn the lights off in the room. If it's not totally dark, gather with the teacher and classmates underneath a blanket, sitting on the floor.
3. Chew the wintergreen mint with his mouth open, watching his classmates chew their mints the same way. Watch the sparkles.

Talk About
• What did God put in the sky at night?
• Do you ever have dreams at night? What do you like to dream about?
• What are some good things you can think about before you go to sleep at night?
• Who took care of the person in our story at night?
• Who takes care of you at night?

Suggested Bible Stories
Creation of the Sun, Moon, and Stars
God's Promise to Abraham
Jacob's Dream
Joseph's Dreams
God Leads Israel With a Pillar of Fire
Gideon
Samuel Hears God
Solomon's Dream
Daniel and the Lions
The Wise Men
Nicodemus Visits Jesus at Night
Paul in a Basket
Peter Escapes From Prison
Paul and Silas in Prison
Paul's Nephew Hears a Plot

Heavy and Light

Materials
kitchen scales
items found around a house (nails, rocks, a shoe, a
  toy, leaves, feathers, a brick, a baseball, a toy
  plastic ball, foods—apple, orange, banana,
  potato)

Guide Each Child To
1. Select two items, holding one in each hand.
2. Tell which she thinks is heavier.
3. Weigh the items and see which is heavier.

Talk About
• Do you have to be stronger to hold some-
thing heavy or something light?
• Name some things you are strong enough
to do.
• What is God strong enough to do?

Suggested Bible Stories
Samson
Through the Roof
Peter Escapes From Prison

Natural Laws

Materials
two sheets of plain white paper
one chair
incline (one long block and a few smaller blocks)
toy car or truck

Guide Each Child To
1. Stand on a chair and drop the paper. Watch what happens.
2. Help build an incline using blocks to prop up one end of the long block.
3. Roll the car or truck down the incline.
4. Make the incline steeper and then less steep, trying the car each time.
5. Watch what happens and how the car moves at different speeds.

Talk About
• Why don't things fall up? Which way do you go if you jump off something? Why?
• Does a toy car go faster down a steep hill or on flat land? Why?
• What rules has God given us? Why? If God doesn't change his rules about the earth (gravity, speed), what about his rules about how we should act?
• We get in trouble if we don't believe and follow God's natural laws (like gravity). We also get in trouble if we don't believe and follow God's other rules.
• Who obeyed or disobeyed in our story? What happened?

Suggested Bible Stories
Adam and Eve Eat the Fruit
The Plagues in Egypt
The Ten Commandments
Twelve Spies
Israelites Wander in the Wilderness
King Josiah Finds God's Word
Jonah
The Wise Man's House
Two Sons and a Vineyard

Block Bed

Materials
blocks

Guide Each Child To
1. Work together to build a child-sized bed out of blocks.
2. Take turns lying on it.
3. Use a block for a pillow.

Talk About
• How does a block bed feel? What kind of bed do you have?
• How does it feel to sleep in a strange bed away from your house?
• Do you ever have dreams?
• What happened while the person in our story was asleep? What kind of bed do you think he was sleeping on?

Suggested Bible Stories
Jacob's Dream
Joseph's Dreams
Pharaoh's Dreams
Samuel Hears God
Joseph, Mary, and Jesus Go to Egypt

Will It Last?

Materials

a variety of objects that can be handled by children (objects that do not last a long time: a banana, balloon, toy, sock, toothbrush)

pillowcase

Guide Each Child To

1. Take a turn pulling one object from the pillowcase.
2. Touch and feel the object, then pass it around to others.

Talk About

• Will this object last forever? What will happen to it someday?

• How about God's love? Will it last forever? God will never stop loving you.

• How did God show his love in our story?

Suggested Bible Stories

Noah
God's Promise to Abraham
Jacob's Dream
Manna and Quail
Hannah Prays for a Baby
Ravens Feed Elijah
The Lost Sheep
The Lost Coin
The Runaway Son
Jesus and the Children
Jesus Washes His Friends' Feet
The Resurrection

Animals Talk and Walk

Materials
none

Guide Each Child To
1. Think of an animal and the sound it makes.
2. Make the animal sound, letting his classmates guess what animal it is.
3. If necessary, give clues about the animal's size, shape, color, and movement.
4. Join his classmates in moving around the room, acting out his animal's movements.
5. Guess his other classmates' animal sounds.

Talk About
- Who made animals?
- Which animal is your favorite? Why?
- What animal was in our story? What happened?

Suggested Bible Stories
Creation of Animals
Noah
Isaac Gets a Wife
Balaam's Talking Donkey
David, the Shepherd Boy
Daniel and the Lions
Jesus Is Born
Tax Money in a Fish
The Lost Sheep
The Triumphal Entry

Sound Waves

Materials
3 feet of cotton clothesline cord
metal spoon
paper towels
table
water

Prepare Ahead of Time
Tie the spoon to the middle of the cord.

Guide Each Child To
1. Choose a partner.
2. Hold one end of the cord to one of her ears. Place her other hand over her other ear. Her partner does the same at the other end of the cord.
3. Bump the spoon on the table or on a chair and listen to the sound. Put the cord and spoon away.
4. Lay her head on a table. Let her partner tap on the table while she listens.

Talk About
• We hear sound when the waves hit our eardrums. What makes things hard to hear? (Distance, barriers between us and the sound.)
• If you want to listen to someone shouting, do you need to be close to him? If you want to hear someone whispering, where do you need to be?
• Why is it important to listen?
• Did someone in the story listen? What did he listen to?

Suggested Bible Stories
Adam and Eve Eat the Fruit
Noah
God's Promise to Abraham
Burning Bush
The Plagues in Egypt
Samuel Hears God
Gabriel Appears to Mary
John the Baptist Is Born
Nicodemus Visits Jesus at Night
Mary and Martha
Philip and the Man From Ethiopia

Music Maker

Materials

one 5-by-5-inch square of tissue paper for each child

one hair comb for each child

Guide Each Child To

1. Fold the tissue paper around the comb, with the teeth of the comb at the fold.
2. Place his lips against the tissue-wrapped comb, with his mouth slightly open.
3. Blow out as he hums the tune "Jesus Loves Me" to make a buzzing melody.
4. Put the comb down and close his mouth, continuing to hum.
5. Feel his throat with his hand as he hums to feel the vibrations.

Talk About

• Why does the comb tickle your lips? (Because the paper is moving back and forth very fast with the sound.) We say it vibrates. That helps to make the buzzing sound.
• Can you feel the vibration in your throat? Your voice comes from the vocal cords in your voice box. The air you use when you sing vibrates your vocal cords.
• What is an instrument? What is your favorite instrument?
• What is your favorite song about God?
• Who worshiped God with songs in our story?

Suggested Bible Stories

Crossing the Red Sea
David Plays the Harp
Singers Lead Jehoshaphat's Army
The Triumphal Entry
Paul and Silas in Prison

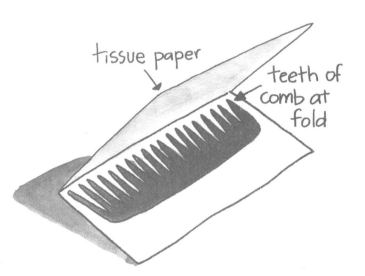

tissue paper

teeth of comb at fold

Balance Beam

Materials

balance beam (set a board 1-by-5-feet long on top of two bricks, one at each end) or blocks laid end-to-end for about 4 feet

Guide Each Child To

Take a turn walking across the balance beam and jumping off.

Talk About

• Why don't you go up when you jump?
• Can you see gravity? Is it real, even if you can't see it? How do you know it's real?
• You don't see God, but he is real. In fact, he created gravity! How did God show the people in our story that he was real? Did they see God? Did they believe?

Suggested Bible Stories

Jacob's Dream
The Plagues in Egypt
Jericho's Walls Fall Down
David and Goliath
Naaman
The Fiery Furnace
Writing on the Wall
Water Into Wine
Jairus's Daughter
Jesus Walks on Water
The Resurrection
Peter Escapes From Prison

Building Higher

Materials

a variety of sizes of blocks

Guide Each Child To

1. Help build a tower by putting a small block at the bottom and the larger blocks on top. Notice how high she can build.
2. Help build a tower with a big block at the bottom and the smaller blocks on top. Notice how high she can build.
3. Build more towers however she wants.

Talk About
- What happened when the small block was on the bottom? Could you build higher when the small block was on the bottom or when the big block was on the bottom?
- Have you ever seen tall, tall houses? Do you live in a tall apartment house?
- What kind of house do you live in? Who gives us houses to live in?
- What did the people in the story build?

Suggested Bible Stories
Noah
Tower of Babel
Israelites Work for Pharaoh
Building the Tabernacle
Solomon Builds the Temple
Elisha's Room on the Roof
Rebuilding Jerusalem's Walls
The Wise Man's House
Bigger Barns

Oil and Water

Materials

transparent jar with a lid
vegetable oil
water

Guide Each Child To

1. Help put water into the jar until it's about one-fourth full.
2. Add vegetable oil until the jar is about half full.
3. Put the lid on the jar.
4. Take a turn shaking the jar. Try to mix the oil and water. Observe what happens after each person shakes it.

Talk About

• Do you think oil and water will mix? What happens when the jar stands still for a minute?
• Who made water? Who made oil?
• What do people use water for? What do people use oil for? (People in Bible times used oil for making light.)
• What did the people in our story use water (or oil) for?

Suggested Bible Stories

Isaac Gets a Wife (water for camels)
Baby Moses
Water From a Rock
David Is Anointed
A Widow Shares With Elijah
A Widow's Oil Jars
John the Baptist
Jesus Is Baptized
Water Into Wine
The Woman at the Well
Jesus Washes His Friends' Feet
Philip and the Man From Ethiopia
Peter and Cornelius
Lydia
Paul and Silas in Prison (jailer is baptized)

Seasonal Smells

Materials

potpourri, candles, or room deodorizers that have seasonal smells:

    spring (fresh flowers, rain shower, meadow)
    summer (citrus, roses)
    fall (pumpkin, spice, wood smoke)
    winter (evergreen, peppermint, cinnamon)

Guide Each Child To

1. Choose a scent and smell it.
2. Tell what that smell reminds him of.
3. Repeat the process with other scents.

Talk About

• Who made smells? Who made your nose so it could smell?
• What kinds of things do you smell in the spring when rain comes and flowers grow?
• What kinds of things do you smell in the winter when it's cold and people build fires in their fireplaces?
• What kinds of food do you like to smell?
• What do you suppose the people in our story smelled?

Suggested Bible Stories

Garden of Eden
Noah
Abraham and the Three Visitors
Birthright and Blessing
Burning Bush
Esther
Daniel Refuses the King's Food
The Fiery Furnace
The Great Catch of Fish
Birds and Flowers (Sermon on the Mount)
Jesus Feeds 5,000
Tax Money in a Fish
Jesus Makes Breakfast for His Friends

Falling

Materials
none

Guide Each Child To
1. Stand in front of his teacher with his back to the teacher.
2. Put his arms at his side and his heels on the floor, keeping his legs straight.
3. Fall backwards, letting his teacher catch him.
4. Try it several times if he needs to, until he can do it comfortably.

Talk About
• I promise to catch you. Do you trust me? Try it and see.
• Now that you've done it once and I caught you, do you trust me? Why? Because I kept my promise.
• God keeps his promises. God says he will take care of you and he will never leave you. Do you trust him?
• Who trusted God in our story? What happened?

Suggested Bible Stories
Abraham Travels
Jacob's Dream
Joseph Leads Egypt
Water From a Rock
Jericho's Walls Fall Down
David and Goliath
Servant Sees God's Army
The Fiery Furnace
Woman Touches Jesus' Hem
Blind Bartimaeus
Peter Escapes From Prison
Paul's Shipwreck

Boiled Egg

Materials
two raw eggs for demonstration
pan, water
one boiled egg for each child
knife for teacher's use
bowl
paper plates, paper towels
stove or hot plate

Prepare Ahead of Time
Boil one egg for each child.

Guide Each Child To
1. Watch the teacher crack open a raw egg and let the insides drop into a bowl.
2. Look at the yolk and the egg white. Sniff it to see if it has a smell.
3. Watch the teacher place the other raw egg in a pan of water, heat the water on the stove, and let it boil gently for 10 minutes.
4. Watch the teacher peel the freshly boiled egg and cut it open. Compare the contents of the boiled egg and the raw egg.
5. Choose a boiled egg to peel and eat.

Talk About
• How are the boiled and raw eggs alike? How are they different?
• What made the difference? (The heat did.) Look what the heat did to the egg. The heat changed it.
• Where does heat come from?
• What is hot in the sky? Some heat comes from the sun. Inside your egg is something that looks like a little round sun. Can you find it? What is it?
• Who made the sun? Who made your egg?

Suggested Bible Stories
Creation of the Sun, Moon, and Stars
Jacob's Dream
The Sun Stands Still
Let Your Light Shine
Paul to Damascus
John Sees Heaven

Magnets

Materials
lots of metal paper clips
several thin paper plates
several magnets

Guide Each Child To
1. Choose a magnet and go around the room finding out what will stick to the magnet.
2. Put some paper clips on a paper plate.
3. Hold a magnet under the plate, touching the plate.
4. Move the magnet around under the plate. Pick up one "leader" paper clip. Then add on more clips.
5. Try to make a long line of paper clips.

Talk About
• What will stick to the magnet?
• Which paper clip is the first one, the "leader" of your line of clips?
• Have you ever been a leader of anything? What does a leader do?
• Who was a leader in our story? What did he do?

Suggested Bible Stories
Joseph Leads Egypt
Crossing the Red Sea (Moses leads)
The Sun Stands Still
Deborah
Gideon
Samson
David Is Anointed
Solomon's Dream
Singers Lead Jehoshaphat's Army
Esther
John the Baptist
Jesus Chooses Twelve Friends
Jesus Washes His Friends' Feet
Philip and the Man From Ethiopia

Bubble Rainbow

Materials
bubble blowing soap
bubble blowing wands
flashlights

Guide Each Child To
1. Choose a partner who will hold a flashlight.
2. Blow bubbles while his partner shines the light on the bubbles.
3. Notice the rainbow colors in the bubbles when the light shines through them.
4. Hold the flashlight while his partner blows bubbles.

Talk About
• Who made rainbows and colors?
• You are sharing with your partner. What do you share at home? What do you share with friends?
• Why does God want us to share?
• Who shared in our story? What happened?

Suggested Bible Stories
Noah
Abraham and the Three Visitors
David and Jonathan
David and Mephibosheth
A Widow Shares With Elijah
Elisha's Room on the Roof
Jesus Feeds 5,000
Perfume on Jesus' Feet

Rainbow Crayons

Materials
old, broken crayons
foil baking cups
aluminum foil
baking sheet
oven
pot holders

Prepare Ahead of Time
Preheat the oven to 350 degrees.

Guide Each Child To
1. Choose a foil baking cup.
2. Place several different colors of broken crayons in her baking cup.
3. Set her baking cup on the baking sheet.
4. Let the teacher set the baking sheet in the 350-degree oven for 3 to 5 minutes, depending on the number of crayons used.
5. Let the teacher take the baking sheet out of the oven. Set the baking cups on a counter or window ledge to cool for 3 to 5 minutes.
6. Pop the rainbow colored crayons out of the baking cups. They are now ready to use.

Talk About
• Who made the rainbow? Who made colors? What is your favorite color?
• What are the colors in your crayon? What else is that color?
• What was colorful in our story? What happened in our story?

Suggested Bible Stories
Creation of Light and Color
Noah
Joseph's Colorful Coat
Birds and Flowers (Sermon on the Mount)
John Sees Heaven

Mixing Colors

Materials
six clear jars with lids (baby food jars work well)
water
red, yellow, and blue liquid tempera paint
plastic spoons
paper towels

Guide Each Child To
1. Help fill the jars half full with water.
2. Help dip a spoonful of red paint into one jar, blue into another jar, and yellow into a third jar.
3. Put the lids on the jars and take turns shaking the jars.
4. Pour a little red and yellow paint into the fourth jar. Shake it to see what happens to the colors.
5. Pour a little blue and yellow paint into the fifth jar. Shake it to see what happens to the colors.
6. Pour a little red and blue paint into the sixth jar. Shake it to see what happens to the colors.

Talk About
• How did the red change when we mixed yellow with it? How did the blue change when we mixed yellow with it? How did the red change when we mixed blue with it?
• Who made colors? Which is your favorite color?
• What else in the world is blue? green? red? yellow? orange? purple?
• What was colorful in our story?

Suggested Bible Stories
Creation of Light and Color
Noah
Joseph's Colorful Coat
Birds and Flowers (Sermon on the Mount)
John Sees Heaven

Translucent or Transparent

Materials
strong flashlight or lamp
construction paper
one piece of plain white paper per child
one transparent plastic page protector per child
newspaper
cotton balls
baby oil

Guide Each Child To
1. Try to shine the light through each kind of material: construction paper, plain white paper, and the page protector. Tell what happens.
2. Lay newspapers on the table to protect it.
3. Get a piece of plain white paper and a cotton ball. Put baby oil on the cotton ball and rub it over the paper. It will become translucent.
4. Try shining the light through each piece of paper again. Tell what happens.

Talk About
• When light shines through something and you can see clearly through it, we say it is transparent. Which page is transparent?
• When light shines through something, but you can't see clearly through it, then it is translucent. Which page is translucent?
• When light won't shine through something, we say it is opaque. Which page is opaque?
• Where did the light come from in our story? What happened?

Suggested Bible Stories
Creation of Light and Color
God Leads Israel With a Pillar of Fire
The Sun Stands Still
Gideon
Paul to Damascus
John Sees Heaven

Pop the Corn

Materials

one ear of corn in the husk
one can of corn
can opener
corn flakes
puffed corn cereal
unpopped popcorn
corn popper or microwave

Guide Each Child To

1. Let the teacher open the can of corn.
2. Examine the different types of corn.
3. Pop the popcorn.
4. Taste some of the different kinds of corn.

Talk About

• When we pop the popcorn, how does it change?
• What makes corn pop? (A tiny bit of water inside the corn kernel expands as it gets hotter, and finally it explodes.)
• Who made food for us to eat? What is your favorite food?
• What did the people in the story eat? What happened?

Suggested Bible Stories

Birthright and Blessing
Manna and Quail
Ruth
Ravens Feed Elijah
A Widow Shares With Elijah
Daniel Refuses the King's Food
John the Baptist
Jesus Feeds 5,000
The Lord's Supper
Jesus Makes Breakfast for His Friends

Pulling

Materials
wagon or wheelbarrow
piece of paper
marker or pen

Prepare Ahead of Time
On the paper, write the directions about how to use the wheelbarrow: 1. Put the wheel on the floor; 2. Holding the handles, lift the feet of the wheelbarrow off the floor; and 3. Push it forward.

Plan to tell the children that you have directions for the wheelbarrow, but you don't want to use them. You want to do it your own way. Then toss the directions aside and turn the wagon or wheelbarrow upside down.

Guide Each Child To
1. Take a turn sitting on the upside down wagon or wheelbarrow with a partner while other children try to pull it.
2. Take a turn pulling the upside down wagon or wheelbarrow with two children sitting on it.
3. Help the teacher figure out why the wagon or wheelbarrow is so hard to pull. (Suggest turning it upright.)
4. Turn the wagon or wheelbarrow upright.
5. Take a turn sitting in the wagon or wheelbarrow with a partner while other children pull it.
6. Take a turn pulling the wagon or wheelbarrow with two children sitting on it.

Talk About
• Do you think it might help to read the directions? (Read the directions.) If I had followed the directions, I could have saved us from some trouble.
• Which is easier: pulling the wagon upside down or right side up? Why is it easier when the wagon is right side up? The wheels make it easier. Wheels make things easier to move.
• God gives us directions or rules or commands to obey. When we follow God's rules, it saves us from a lot of trouble.
• What are some of God's rules? How do you obey at home? How do you obey in our classroom?
• Who obeyed (or disobeyed) in our story? What happened?

Suggested Bible Stories
Adam and Eve Eat the Fruit
Abraham Travels
The Ten Commandments
Ravens Feed Elijah
King Josiah Finds God's Word
Daniel Refuses the King's Food
Jonah
The Great Catch of Fish
Two Sons and a Vineyard

Sink or Float

Materials
various household items and toys that will not be
    damaged if immersed in water
one bucket
water

Guide Each Child To
1. Help fill the bucket with water.
2. Take a turn placing an item in the water to see if
it sinks or floats.

Talk About
• Which items sink? Why do you think they
sink?
• Which items float? Why do you think they
float?
• There was lots of water in our story. What
happened?

Suggested Bible Stories
Noah
Crossing the Red Sea
Jonah
Jesus Stills the Storm
Jesus Walks on Water
Paul's Shipwreck

Paper Jail

Materials
plain white paper
scissors

Guide Each Child To watch as you:
1. Fold a piece of plain white paper in half horizontally. See the illustration.
2. Cut out a section of the fold as shown (about 1 by 6½ inches).
3. With the paper folded, make eight evenly spaced cuts from the edges of the cut-out window to within 1 inch of the edge of the paper.
4. From the edge of the paper, make seven evenly spaced cuts that go between the previous cuts to within 1 inch of the edge of the window.
5. Point out how small the folded paper is. Then unfold, shake out, and let the children take turns stepping through the hole. Something small turned out to be big.

Talk About while you cut:
• What is a jail? Let's cut some jail bars into this piece of paper.
• Who was in jail in our story? What happened?
• Can you walk through these jail bars? Let's try. (Unfold the paper and walk through.)

Suggested Bible Stories
Joseph in Prison
Peter Escapes From Prison
Paul and Silas in Prison
Paul's Nephew Hears a Plot

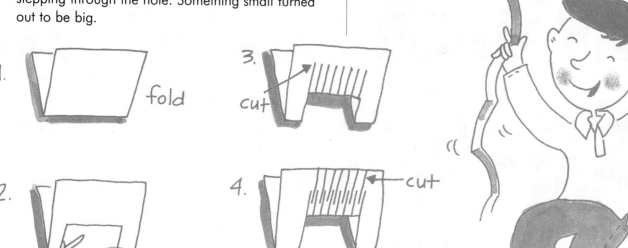

1. fold

2. cut

3. cut

4. cut

Push a Box

Materials
big box
heavy objects like big books

Guide Each Child To
1. Help fill the box with heavy objects.
2. Watch as the smallest child tries to push the box across the room.
3. Watch as the next smallest child joins the first child to help try to push the box.
4. Join his classmates as, one by one, smallest to biggest, they join the children helping to push the box.

Talk About
• Why wouldn't the box move at first? When did it start moving? What happened when more children joined in to help?
• Prayer is getting help from the strongest, smartest friend you have. Whom do we pray to?
• What can we pray about? When can we pray? Where can we pray?
• Who prayed in our story? What happened?

Suggested Bible Stories
Isaac Gets a Wife
Hannah Prays for a Baby
David Plays the Harp (Psalms)
Elijah on Mt. Carmel
Singers Lead Jehoshaphat's Army
The Lord's Prayer
A Pharisee and a Tax Collector Pray
Peter Escapes From Prison
Paul and Silas in Prison

Fire Safety

Materials

book about fire safety (like *Survival Skills*, Lucy Smith, Usborne Books) or an article about fire safety from an encyclopedia

Prepare Ahead of Time

Read about fire safety and be familiar with the rules. Review the fire escape route from your classroom so that you can teach it to the children. Practice the way you will tell it so that the children are not frightened, but have fun and become aware.

Guide Each Child To

1. Follow the teacher in a fire drill to learn the fire escape route from her classroom.
2. Listen and watch as the teacher shows some fire safety procedures.
3. Practice some of the fire safety procedures.

Talk About

• Who takes care of you always? Will God ever leave you?
• It's wise for us to know how to stay safe, but if we are ever in trouble, we can talk to God. Why would we want to talk to God if we have any kind of trouble?
• Who saw the fire in our story? What happened?

Suggested Bible Stories

Burning Bush
God Leads Israel With a Pillar of Fire
Gideon
Elijah on Mt. Carmel
The Fiery Furnace
Paul on Malta

Measuring

Materials
different sizes of gloves
rulers or measuring tapes

Guide Each Child To
Measure each glove from its cuff to the tip of the middle finger.

Talk About
• Which person in a family might wear this glove? How long is it? Is there a glove that's longer than this one? Which one is shorter?
• Do the people in your family have gloves? When do they wear them?
• Who gave us our families?
• Who were the people in the family in our story?

Suggested Bible Stories
Adam and Eve Have a Family
Isaac Is Born
Jacob and Esau
Joseph's Brothers Go to Egypt
Baby Moses
Ruth
A Widow's Oil Jars
Peter's Mother-in-Law
Jairus's Daughter
The Runaway Son
Two Sons and a Vineyard

Big and Little Clothes

Materials

shoes of different sizes
gloves of different sizes
socks of different sizes
T-shirts of different sizes
measuring tapes
rulers

Guide Each Child To

1. Help put the shoes in order from smallest to largest or largest to smallest.
2. Help put the gloves in order from smallest to largest or largest to smallest.
3. Help put the socks in order from smallest to largest or largest to smallest.
4. Help put the T-shirts in order from smallest to largest or largest to smallest.
5. Use the measuring tape or ruler to measure a shoe, a glove, a sock, and a T-shirt of her choice.

Talk About
• Which people in your family are smaller than you? Which people are bigger than you?
• You were smaller one time. What happened? What happens to your clothes when you grow bigger?
• Who was the child (young person) in our story? What did he do?
• What can you do to help?

Suggested Bible Stories
Joseph's Dreams
Baby Moses
Samuel's New Coats
Samuel Hears God
David, the Shepherd Boy
David and Goliath
Naaman (servant girl)
Jesus as a Boy in the Temple
Jairus's Daughter
Jesus Feeds 5,000
Jesus and the Children
Paul's Nephew Hears a Plot

Cooking

Hot Chocolate Mix

Ingredients
8-quart box of powdered milk
2 cups of powdered coffee creamer
8 ounces of instant chocolate drink powder
½ cup of powdered sugar
very warm water, not hot

Kitchen Tools
large bowl
mixing spoon
measuring cups
Styrofoam hot cups
plastic spoons

Guide Each Child To
1. Help measure and mix the powdered milk, coffee creamer, chocolate powder, and powdered sugar in a bowl.
2. Dip ⅓ cup of mix into a Styrofoam cup.
3. Add very warm (not hot) water to make the cup two-thirds full.
4. Stir and drink.

Talk About
• Let's thank God before we drink our hot chocolate.
• What's your favorite thing to drink?
• What's your favorite thing to eat?
• Why do we thank God for our food and drink?
• Who was thankful in our story? What were they thankful for?

Suggested Bible Stories
Noah

Isaac Gets a Wife (Rebekah waters servant's camels)

Chicken Noodle Soup

Ingredients
pre-cooked, canned chicken chunks
4 cups of water
4 teaspoons instant chicken bouillon
2 carrots, sliced into disks
1 teaspoon basil
3 to 4 ounces of noodles

Kitchen Tools
soup pot
bowls, spoons
measuring cups, spoons
mixing spoon
ladle or serving spoon

Guide Each Child To
1. Help put water in the soup pot.
2. Add bouillon, chicken chunks, carrots, and basil.
3. Bring the soup to a boil, then turn it to simmer. Cook the soup for 10 minutes, stirring occasionally.
4. Add noodles and cook the soup for 10 more minutes.
5. Pour the soup into bowls and allow it to cool a bit. (Putting an ice cube in each bowl of soup for a minute helps to cool it quickly.)

Talk About
• We're sharing our soup. What else can you share?
• How do you feel when someone shares with you?
• Who shared in our story?
• Why does God want us to share?

Suggested Bible Stories
Abraham and the Three Visitors
Birthright and Blessing
Ruth
David and Jonathan
David and Mephibosheth
Elisha's Room on the Roof
Jesus Feeds 5,000
Jesus Makes Breakfast for His Friends
Lydia

Fruity Cream Cheese Sandwiches

Ingredients
soft cream cheese
fresh, washed seedless red and green grapes
thin-sliced wheat bread

Kitchen Tools
knife for teacher's use
mixing bowl, spoon
paper plates, plastic knives
paper towels

Prepare Ahead of Time
Cut the grapes in half.

Guide Each Child To
1. Help put the cream cheese into a bowl.
2. Add grapes and stir to mix.
3. Dip some of the mix onto a piece of bread and spread it with a plastic knife.
4. Place another slice of bread on top.
5. Put the sandwich on a paper plate and eat it.

Talk About
• What do grapes grow on? What do they look like when they are hanging on the vine? (You may want to show a bunch of grapes.)
• What do grapes taste like? Did you ever taste grape jelly, grape Popsicles, or grape juice?
• Somebody grew grapes or found grapes in our story. Tell about what happened.

Suggested Bible Stories
Twelve Spies
Two Sons and the Vineyard

English Muffin Animals

Ingredients
2 English muffin halves for each child
soft margarine
raisins

Kitchen Tools
toaster
plastic knives
paper plates

Guide Each Child To
1. Toast two English muffin halves and put margarine on them.
2. Place the English muffin halves on a paper plate.
3. Cut one of the muffin halves in half to make two semicircles.
4. Arrange the muffin halves to be a dog, rabbit, or fish as shown.
5. Place raisins on the animal shapes to make eyes, nose, and mouth.

Talk About
- What kind of animal do you like best?
- Do you have an animal at your house?
- How do you take care of your animal?
- What kind of animal was in our story? What happened?

Suggested Bible Stories
Creation of Animals
Noah
Isaac Gets a Wife
Balaam's Talking Donkey
Saul Looks for Lost Donkeys
Jonah
The Great Catch of Fish
Tax Money in a Fish
Jesus Makes Breakfast for His Friends

Dog

Fish

Rabbit

Rainbow Cake

Ingredients
pound cake or white sheet cake, unfrosted
one 12-ounce tub of whipped topping
1 pint of strawberries, cut into halves
1 pint of blueberries
about 12 peach slices, cut into chunks
2 kiwifruit, cut into chunks

Kitchen Tools
paper plates, paper towels
plastic knives, forks

Guide Each Child To
1. Help frost the cake with the whipped topping.
2. Help arrange the different colors of fruit across the cake in an arch to form a rainbow. Put blueberries across the top in the first row, kiwifruit in the second row, peaches in the next row, and strawberries in the last row.
3. Help cut a piece of cake for herself and put it on her plate.

Talk About
• Did you ever see a rainbow in the sky? What was it like?
• When do rainbows come into the sky?
• What color do you like best?
• What was colorful in our story? What happened?

Suggested Bible Stories
Noah
Joseph's Colorful Coat
Jonah
Jesus Stills the Storm
John Sees Heaven (rainbow around the throne, Revelation 4)

Treasure Salad

Ingredients
4 packages of gelatin (one red, one yellow,
one green, one blue)

Kitchen Tools
plastic knives, spoons
pancake turner
bowls

Prepare Ahead of Time
Make four bowls of gelatin, one of each color. Use
wide bowls or pans so that the gelatin will be about
1-inch deep.

Guide Each Child To
1. Help cut the gelatin, making lines to form
1-inch cubes.
2. Help scoop the gelatin out of each pan onto a
plate using a pancake turner. Put one color of
gelatin cubes on each plate.
3. Get a bowl and spoon and scoop two of each
color of gelatin cube into his bowl.

Talk About
• What's a treasure? What are jewels?
• Did you ever see sparkly jewels or fancy
jewelry? Where? What was it like?
• What were the treasures, riches, or jewels in
our story?

Suggested Bible Stories
Isaac Gets a Wife
Solomon Builds the Temple
Esther
Hidden Treasure

Arrow Cheese Toast

Ingredients
1 piece of bread for each child
one-half slice of American processed cheese for
  each child

Kitchen Tools
toaster oven or broiler
pot holders
baking sheet
paper plates and towels

Guide Each Child To
1. Slice each square of cheese into rectangles and triangles as shown.
2. Arrange the square and triangles on the bread to make an arrow as shown.
3. Let the teacher broil the toast until the cheese starts melting.

Talk About
• People used to fight with bows and arrows. Who was fighting in our story? Who won?
• How did God take care of the people in our story? How does God take care of you?

Suggested Bible Stories
Jericho's Walls Fall Down
Deborah
Gideon
David and Jonathan
Servant Sees God's Army
Singers Lead Jehoshaphat's Army

cut cheese slice like this

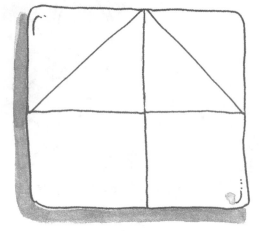

arrange to form arrow.

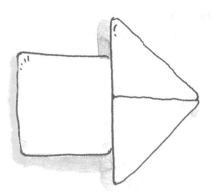

Kiss Cookies

Ingredients
1 roll of refrigerated peanut butter cookie dough
chocolate kiss candies

Kitchen Tools
table knife
baking sheet
oven
aluminum foil
pot holders
paper towels

Prepare Ahead of Time
Preheat the oven to the temperature recommended
on the package of dough.

Guide Each Child To
1. Slice off some dough.
2. Pat her dough into a circle on a piece of foil.
3. Unwrap a candy kiss and put it in the middle of
her cookie.
4. Place her piece of foil on the baking sheet.
5. Let the teacher bake it according to the package
instructions.

Talk About
• Whom do you love? Who loves you?
• Who are some people you love in your
family? Who are some friends you love?
• How can you show somebody you love
them?
• Who were the people in our story who
loved (and helped) each other?

Suggested Bible Stories
Adam and Eve Have a Family
Isaac Gets a Wife
Jacob and Rachel
Ruth
Esther

Ham Rolls

Ingredients (for 24 rolls)
two 5-ounce cans of chopped ham
2 cups of grated cheddar or Colby cheese
3 tablespoons mustard
4 tablespoons stick margarine, melted
2 dozen brown-and-serve rolls

Kitchen Tools
plastic knives
bowl or pan for melting margarine
mixing bowl, spoon
baking sheet
pot holders
measuring cups, spoons
paper plates

Prepare Ahead of Time
Preheat the oven to 400 degrees.
   Melt the margarine (30 to 40 seconds on high in a microwave).

Guide Each Child To
1. Help mix the ham, cheese, mustard, and margarine in a bowl.
2. Break a roll in half.
3. Spread the ham and cheese mixture between the halves.
4. Bake the rolls at 400 degrees for 7 minutes.

Talk About
• Who gives us our food?
• What is your favorite food?
• What kind of food did the person in our story have?

Suggested Bible Stories
Abraham and the Three Visitors
Joseph's Brothers Go to Egypt
Manna and Quail
Ruth
Ravens Feed Elijah
Esther
Daniel Refuses the King's Food
Jesus Feeds 5,000
Paul's Shipwreck

Chocolate Cherry Bird Nests

Ingredients (for about 4 dozen)
¾ cup sugar
⅔ cup softened margarine
2 eggs
1 teaspoon vanilla
one 6-ounce package chocolate chips
2 cups uncooked oats
1½ cups flour
1 teaspoon baking powder
¼ teaspoon salt
two 10-ounce jars maraschino cherries

Kitchen Tools
mixing bowl, spoon
electric mixer
measuring cups, spoons
microwave oven
conventional oven
baking sheet
pot holders

Prepare Ahead of Time
Preheat the oven to 350 degrees.

Guide Each Child To
1. Help put sugar, margarine, eggs, and vanilla into the mixing bowl. (Beat until smooth.)
2. Help melt the chocolate chips in a microwave on high for about 2 minutes, stirring halfway through.
3. Mix the melted chips into the sugar mixture.
4. Stir in the oats, flour, baking powder, and salt.
5. Drop a heaping teaspoon of dough onto an ungreased baking sheet.
6. Push one cherry down into the middle of the dough. The dough is the nest, the cherry is the egg in the nest.
7. Bake for 12 minutes at 350 degrees.

Talk About
• Where do you see birds?
• Did you ever see a bird's nest? What did it look like?
• Where are some other places birds might live?
• Tell about the bird(s) in our story.

Suggested Bible Stories
Creation of Animals
Noah
Ravens Feed Elijah
Jesus Is Baptized
Birds and Flowers (Sermon on the Mount)

Apple Honey Nutters

Ingredients
½ cup of peanut butter
¼ cup wheat germ
¼ cup nonfat dry milk
2 tablespoons honey
1 apple for every two children

Kitchen Tools
knife for teacher's use
mixing bowl, spoon
measuring spoons, cups
plastic spoons
paper plates, towels

Guide Each Child To
1. Help measure and mix the peanut butter, wheat germ, dry milk, and honey.
2. Watch the teacher cut the apples in half and scoop out the core.
3. Fill the center of the apple with the peanut butter mixture and spread it over the apple.
4. Place the apple on a paper plate and eat the apple honey nutter.

Talk About
• How did you help to make these apple snacks?
• Why do we need to help each other?
• How do you help at home? How do you help in class?
• Who was a helper in our story? What happened?

Suggested Bible Stories
Adam and Eve Have a Family
Isaac Gets a Wife (Rebekah gives water to the camels)
Baby Moses (Miriam watches and helps)
Ruth
The Good Samaritan
Mary and Martha
Jesus Makes Breakfast for His Friends
Dorcas

Sweet Potatoes With Cinnamon

Ingredients

one 15-ounce can sweet potatoes, drained
one 20-ounce can cooked apples, drained
2 tablespoons sugar
½ teaspoon cinnamon
1 tablespoon margarine

Kitchen Tools

baking dish or casserole dish
pot holders
conventional or microwave oven
measuring spoons
mixing bowl, spoon
paper plates or bowls
plastic spoons or forks

Prepare Ahead of Time

Preheat the oven to 375 degrees.

Guide Each Child To

1. Help mix the potatoes, apples, sugar, and cinnamon in a bowl.
2. Pour the potato and apple mixture into the dish.
3. Dot the top of the mixture with margarine.
4. Let the teacher bake it at 375 degrees for 20 minutes, or microwave on high for 5 to 6 minutes, rotating halfway through.
5. Spoon some potatoes and apples onto a plate and let them cool before eating.

Talk About

• When a farmer brings in the fruits and vegetables from the field, we call that "harvest" time. Did you ever grow fruits or vegetables? What did you grow?
• When the farmer brings in the fruits and vegetables, it's a good time to say thank-you to God. Why would a farmer say thank-you to God?
• What can you thank God for?
• How do we say thank-you to God?
• Who said thank-you in our story?

Suggested Bible Stories

Pharaoh's Dreams
Ruth
Solomon Builds the Temple
Jesus Feeds 5,000
Ten Lepers

Moon Cookies

Ingredients
1 roll of refrigerated sugar cookie dough
3 cups powdered sugar
⅛ teaspoon salt
¼ teaspoon orange extract
3½ to 4 tablespoons orange juice

Kitchen Tools
table knife
baking sheet
pot holders
oven
plastic spoons, paper plates
paper towels
sifter
mixing bowl, spoon

Guide Each Child To
1. Help slice the cookie dough and bake it according to the package directions.
2. While cookies are baking, sift the powdered sugar into bowl.
3. Add the salt, orange extract, and orange juice to the sugar. Stir to mix well.
4. When the cookies are done, use a spoon to drizzle the glaze over the cookies.

Talk About
• When do you see the moon? Did you ever see the moon in the daytime?
• What other lights are in the sky?
• Is the moon always big and round? What shapes can it be?
• Who made the moon?
• It was nighttime in our story. What happened that night?

Suggested Bible Stories
Creation of Sun, Moon, and Stars
Jacob's Dream
Joseph's Dreams
The Sun Stands Still
Gideon
Nicodemus Visits Jesus at Night

Apple Wheel Pancakes

Ingredients (for twelve 4½-inch pancakes)
1 cup flour
2 teaspoons baking powder
2 tablespoons sugar
1 egg, beaten
1 cup milk
2 tablespoons vegetable oil
2 to 3 apples
¼ cup sugar
½ teaspoon cinnamon
cooking spray

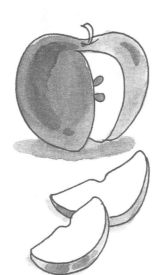

Kitchen Tools
mixing bowl, spoon
knife for teacher's use
measuring spoons, cups
electric skillet
pancake turner
small bowl
plastic spoon, forks
paper plates, towels

Guide Each Child To
1. Help mix flour, baking powder, sugar, egg, milk, and vegetable oil in a bowl.
2. Watch the teacher cut the apples into thin slices.
3. Spray the skillet or griddle with cooking spray and heat it.
4. Pour ¼ cup batter onto the hot skillet.
5. Quickly place apple slices on batter to look like spokes on a wheel.

6. Watch the teacher turn the pancake when the underside is browned and remove the pancake when the apple side is browned.
7. Mix sugar and cinnamon in a small bowl.
8. Sprinkle the sugar and cinnamon mixture on a pancake and eat.

Talk About
- How do people ride to different places?
- What kinds of rides go on wheels?
- Where do you like to ride?
- What's a chariot? What's a cart?
- Who rode in a cart or chariot in our story?

Suggested Bible Stories
Deborah
Solomon Builds the Temple
Elijah Goes Up to Heaven
Servant Sees God's Army
Philip and the Man From Ethiopia

Cheese Logs

Ingredients (for 14 logs)
one 8-ounce box of cream cheese, well-chilled
12 saltine crackers
one 2-ounce jar of bacon bits

Kitchen Tools
one plastic sandwich bag
knife for teacher's use
mixing bowl, spoon
paper plates, towels

Guide Each Child To
1. Help the teacher slice the brick of cream cheese lengthwise into seven slices. Cut each of the seven slices in half.
2. Put the crackers into the sandwich bag and crush them.
3. Mix the cracker crumbs and bacon bits in a bowl.
4. Cover the bottom of a paper plate with the crumb mixture.
5. Roll a "log" of cream cheese in the crumb mixture. (As it is rolled in the crumbs it becomes easier to handle and lengthens into a longer roll like a small log.)
6. Put his log onto a paper plate and eat it.

Talk About
- What's a log? What is it used for?
- How does a house get built?
- What did the people build in our story? What happened?

Suggested Bible Stories
Noah
Tower of Babel
Solomon Builds the Temple
Elisha's Room on the Roof
Rebuilding Jerusalem's Walls

Corn Cake Lions

Ingredients
(for about eight 3-inch corn cake lions)
1 teaspoon salt
1 teaspoon sugar
1 egg
2 teaspoon baking powder
¼ cup flour
1 cup milk
corn meal
cooking spray
raisins

Kitchen Tools
mixing bowl
electric skillet or griddle
mixing spoon
pancake turner
wooden spoon
paper plates
measuring cups, spoons
paper towels

Prepare Ahead of Time
Heat the skillet to a medium high temperature.

Guide Each Child To
1. Help mix egg, sugar, baking powder, and salt together.
2. Add flour and milk, and stir.
3. Mix in corn meal until it is as thick as pancake batter.
4. Spray the skillet with cooking spray.
5. Put ¼ cup batter onto the skillet to cook like a pancake, but immediately after pouring a circle of batter, use a spoon to gently draw out the batter from the center to make spikes like a mane.
6. Put raisins onto the corn cake to make eyes for the lion.
7. Let the teacher turn the corn cake over and brown the other side.
8. Pray and then eat.

Talk About
• Why do we pray before we eat? When else can we pray?
• What can we talk to God about? Where can we pray?
• Who saw a lion in our story? What happened?

Suggested Bible Stories
Creation of Animals
Noah
Samson
David, the Shepherd Boy (kills a lion)
Daniel and the Lions

Fruit Pies

Ingredients
refrigerated crescent roll dough
canned sliced peaches
sugar and cinnamon (optional)

Kitchen Tools
waxed paper
can opener
cookie sheet
fork
foil
paper towels
oven
pot holder or oven mitt

Guide Each Child To
1. Flatten dough (not too thin) for one roll on waxed paper.
2. Place one or two peach slices in the center of the dough.
3. Sprinkle sugar and cinnamon over the peaches.
4. Fold the dough around the peaches, sealing it by pinching it on all sides.
5. Let the teacher bake the pies according to directions on the can of dough.
6. Let the pie cool before eating.

Talk About
• A cook has to wait patiently. What does he have to wait for?
• How can we wait patiently? Can we do something while we are waiting? Can we clean up?
• How does God want us to wait? If you are complaining while you are waiting, does the time go faster? Does it make you feel better? Who had to wait in our story?

Suggested Bible Stories
Abraham and the Three Visitors
Jacob and Rachel
Joseph in Prison
Israelites Wander in the Wilderness
Anna and Simeon

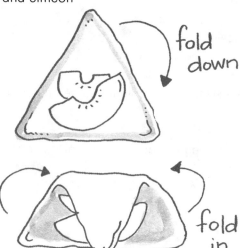

fold down

fold in

Happy Face Cookies

Ingredients (for about 4 dozen)
½ cup margarine
½ teaspoon vanilla
½ cup peanut butter
½ cup brown sugar
½ cup sugar
1 egg
1¼ cups flour
¾ teaspoon soda
¼ teaspoon salt
cocktail peanuts

Kitchen Tools
electric mixer
oven
mixing spoon
measuring cups, spoon
large bowl, small bowl
paper towels
spatula
cookie sheets
oven mitt or pot holders

Prepare Ahead of Time
Preheat the oven to 375 degrees.

Guide Each Child To
1. Help cream the margarine, peanut butter, sugar, egg, and vanilla.
2. Help mix the flour, soda, and salt in the small bowl.
3. Add the dry mixture to the large bowl of the peanut butter mixture.
4. Flatten a tablespoon of dough on a cookie sheet. Press peanuts in the dough to form two eyes and a smile.
5. Let the teacher bake the cookies for 10 minutes.

Talk About
• What makes you joyful? Does it make you joyful to help others?
• When someone loves you, does it give you joy? Who loves you?
• How can you tell someone feels joyful? Who was joyful in our story? Why? What happened?

Suggested Bible Stories
Isaac Is Born
Jacob and Esau
Hannah Prays for a Baby
The Lost Sheep
The Lost Coin
The Runaway Son

Barley Soup

Ingredients
canned beef consommé or beef broth
water
barley

Kitchen Tools
pan
hot plate or stove
spoon
Styrofoam cups
can opener
paper towels

Guide Each Child To
1. Help pour the soup into the pan.
2. Help add one can of water to the soup.
3. Look at and feel the barley.
4. Help add about ⅓ cup of barley to the soup.
5. Wait while the soup is brought to a boil, then simmers on reduced heat for 30 minutes.

Talk About
• Explain that barley is a grain grown in fields. What does the barley look like? Have you ever had barley before? How does it feel? Does it smell like anything before it is cooked?
• How does the soup smell?
• What other kinds of soup have you eaten before?
• Who gives us our food?

Suggested Bible Stories
Joseph's Dreams
Pharaoh's Dreams
Joseph's Brothers Go to Egypt
Ruth
Bigger Barns
The Wheat and the Weeds

Biscuit Sheep

Ingredients
canned refrigerated biscuit dough (1½ biscuits for each child)
flour

 body

Kitchen Tools
aluminum foil
baking sheet
knife for teacher's use
paper plates
scissors
paper towels

 head

legs and tail

Prepare Ahead of Time
Cut the foil into 6-inch squares.
Preheat oven to temperature recommended on the package of dough. Cut half of the biscuits into fourths.

Guide Each Child To
1. Take a piece of foil to work on.
2. Take one dough biscuit and two fourths of another biscuit.
3. Place the whole biscuit in the center of his piece of foil to make the sheep's body.
4. Roll one of the fourths into a ball and flatten it, placing it at one of the upper sides of the body as shown.
5. Divide the other fourth into three parts. Place one part at the end to make a tail and the other two parts at the bottom to make legs as shown.
6. Place his foil with the biscuit sheep on it on the baking sheet.
7. Bake according to the time and temperature recommended on the package of dough.

Talk About
• Have you ever seen real sheep? What are they like?
• Who takes care of the sheep? Who takes care of you?
• Who took care of sheep in our story?

Suggested Bible Stories
Abraham and Lot
Jacob and Rachel
David, the Shepherd Boy
David Plays the Harp (Psalms)
Angels Appear to the Shepherds
The Lost Sheep

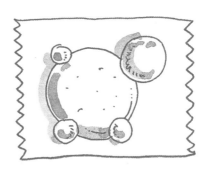

Giant Cookie

Ingredients

¾ cup margarine
½ cup sugar
1½ cups brown sugar
2 eggs
1 teaspoon vanilla
cooking spray

2½ cups flour
1 teaspoon soda
¾ teaspoon salt
1 teaspoon cinnamon
12 ounces chocolate
  chips

Kitchen Tools

electric mixer
measuring cups, spoons
large bowl
large pizza pan

small bowl
oven
mixing spoons
pot holders

Prepare Ahead of Time

Set the margarine out to soften. Preheat the oven to
350 degrees.

Guide Each Child To

1. Help beat the margarine, sugar, and brown
sugar in the large bowl.
2. Add eggs and vanilla and beat some more.
3. In the small bowl, mix flour, soda, salt, and
cinnamon.
4. Add the flour mixture to the margarine and
sugar mixture. Beat it.
5. Stir in the chocolate chips.
6. Spray a pizza pan with cooking spray.
7. Spread the dough on the pizza pan.
8. Bake 12 minutes 350 degrees.

Talk About

• We have only one cookie. Who should get
it? How can we all have some?
• You can share your food. What else can
you share? Why does God want us to share?
• Who shared in our story? What did they
share?

Suggested Bible Stories

Abraham and the Three Visitors
David and Jonathan
A Widow Shares With Elijah
Elisha's Room on the Roof
Jesus Feeds 5,000

Honey Pops

Ingredients
½ cup honey
¼ cup margarine
1 bag unseasoned, unpopped microwave popcorn
1 cup unsalted peanuts

Kitchen Tools
microwave
pot holders
microwaveable pan
paper plates
large mixing bowl
paper towels
mixing spoon
sandwich bags
baking pan
gift wrap curling ribbon
oven

Prepare Ahead of Time
Preheat the oven to 350 degrees.

Guide Each Child To
1. Help microwave the popcorn and pour it into the large bowl.
2. Add the peanuts to the popcorn and stir.
3. Help heat the honey and margarine in the microwave until the margarine is melted. Stir.
4. Stir while pouring the honey and margarine mixture over the popcorn and peanut mixture. Stir until well coated.
5. Spread the mixture onto the baking pan.
6. Bake for 5 to 10 minutes or until crisp.
7. Eat some honey pops and put some in a sandwich bag to give to someone at home. Tie curling ribbon around the bag to decorate the gift.

Talk About
- Who do you plan to give your gift to?
- Why does God want us to be cheerful givers?
- Who gave a gift in our story? What did they give? What happened?

Suggested Bible Stories
Isaac Gets a Wife
Joseph's Colorful Coat
Samuel's New Coats
David and Jonathan
A Widow Shares With Elijah
The Wise Men
Jesus Feeds 5,000
Perfume on Jesus' Feet
The Widow's Mite

Honey Crunch Bananas

Ingredients
half of 1 banana for each child
honey
wheat germ

Kitchen Tools
plastic knives
baking sheet
paper plates
bowl
toothpicks
paper towels

Guide Each Child To
1. Help spread wheat germ on the bottom of one baking pan.
2. Pour honey into the bowl.
3. Peel and slice her banana on her plate.
4. Stick a toothpick into a banana slice.
5. Dip the banana slice into honey and then roll it around in the wheat germ.
6. Do this with each banana slice.

Talk About
• Who gives us food to eat? That's one way God blesses us. Blessings are the good things that God gives us.
• How does this food taste? Is it crunchy? Is it soft? What part of your body tastes this food? Your tongue is one of the blessings God gives you.
• What part of your body smells this food? How does it smell? Your nose is one of the blessings God gives you.
• What other blessings has God given you? What was the blessing in our story?

Suggested Bible Stories
Creation of People
Isaac Is Born
Birthright and Blessing
Joseph's Colorful Coat
Manna and Quail
Ravens Feed Elijah
Elisha's Room on the Roof
Jesus Feeds 5,000
Tax Money in a Fish
Jesus and the Children
Perfume on Jesus' Feet
Dorcas

Cinnamon Angels

Ingredients (for 8 children)
1 refrigerated pan of pie crust dough
¼ cup sugar
½ teaspoon cinnamon

Kitchen Tools

waxed paper	measuring spoons
paper plates	baking sheet
plastic knives	mixing spoon
paper towels	oven
small bowl	pot holders
aluminum foil	

Prepare Ahead of Time

Gently remove the pie crust from the pan and lay it on a piece of waxed paper to form a big, flat circle. Cut the circle of dough into eight wedges like a pie.

Preheat the oven to the temperature recommended on the pie crust package. Tear off an 8-inch piece of aluminum foil for each child.

Guide Each Child To

1. Choose a wedge of pie dough and gently place it on a piece of aluminum foil.
2. Cut the wedge of dough into pieces as shown.
3. Arrange his dough pieces as shown to make an angel.
4. Help measure and mix the cinnamon and sugar in the bowl.
5. Sprinkle cinnamon and sugar over his angel dough.

6. Bake according to the time and temperature recommended on the package.

Talk About
• What do you think an angel looks like?
• Who saw the angel in our story? What happened?

Suggested Bible Stories
Jacob's Dream
Samson
Daniel and the Lions
Gabriel Appears to Mary
John the Baptist Is Born
Angels Appear to the Shepherds
The Resurrection
Jesus Goes Back to Heaven
Peter Escapes From Prison
John Sees Heaven

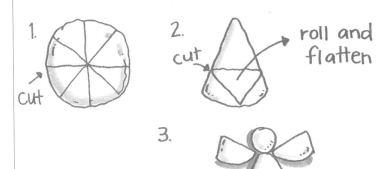

1. cut
2. cut / roll and flatten
3. arrange

Cooperation Cookies

Ingredients (for 2 children)
2 tablespoons honey
2 tablespoons peanut butter
1 cup crisp rice cereal

Kitchen Tools
disposable plastic bowls
waxed paper
measuring cups, spoons
paper plates
plastic spoons
paper towels

Guide Each Child To
1. Choose a friend to work with.
2. With her friend, get a bowl, a spoon, and a piece of waxed paper.
3. Work with her friend, mixing the honey and peanut butter in their bowl.
4. With her friend, add 1 cup crisp rice cereal and stir until the cereal is well coated.
5. Help her friend put spoonfuls of this mixture onto the waxed paper.
6. Help her friend get plates for their cookies.

Talk About
• How did you and your friend help each other? What are some other ways you can help your friends?
• Who are some of your friends? Who gives us good friends?
• Who were the good friends in our story? How did they help each other?

Suggested Bible Stories
Creation of People
Ruth
David and Jonathan
Elijah Goes Up to Heaven
Daniel Refuses the King's Food
The Fiery Furnace
Jesus Chooses Twelve Friends
Through the Roof
Paul in a Basket
Paul and Silas in Prison

Heavenly Fruit Snack

Ingredients
3 teaspoons instant vanilla pudding mix for
    each child
¼ cup milk for each child
graham cracker crumbs
frozen berries (strawberries or blueberries), thawed
half of 1 banana for each child
1 can refrigerated whipped cream
1 maraschino cherry for each child

Kitchen Tools
measuring cups, spoons
plastic spoons, knives
paper plates
paper towels
bowl
paper cups and clear plastic disposable cups

Prepare Ahead of Time
Thaw the frozen berries and put them in a bowl.

Guide Each Child To
1. Pour ¼ cup milk into his paper cup.
2. Add 3 teaspoons of pudding mix to his milk and
stir well.
3. Peel and slice his half of banana on his plate.
4. Place one spoonful of his pudding into his clear
cup.

5. On top of the pudding, put a spoonful of
graham cracker crumbs, a spoonful of berries, and
a few banana slices.
6. Squirt some whipped cream on top.
7. Layer these same ingredients one more time and
add a cherry on top.

Talk About
• What is your favorite thing to eat? Some
people say, "It's delicious!" Others say,
"Mmmm! This is heavenly!" What do they
mean? They mean it's wonderful.
• Name some things that you think are won-
derful. Heaven is even more wonderful!
• What is Heaven like?

Suggested Bible Stories
Elijah Goes Up to Heaven
The Lord's Prayer
The Wise Man's House
Jesus Goes Back to Heaven
John Sees Heaven

Egg Salad Sandwich

Ingredients
3 to 4 hard boiled eggs
1 to 2 tablespoons chopped green olives
1 to 2 tablespoons mayonnaise
bread

Kitchen Tools
knife for teacher's use
mixing spoon
cutting board
plastic knives
bowl
paper plates
fork
paper towels
measuring spoon

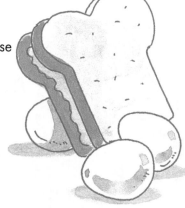

Prepare Ahead of Time
Boil the eggs, chop the green olives, and cut each slice of bread in half.

Guide Each Child To
1. Help take the shells off the eggs and separate the yolks from the whites.
2. Mash the yolks in the bowl using the fork.
3. Add mayonnaise and olives and stir.
4. Watch the teacher chop the egg whites into small chunks.
5. Add the chopped egg whites to the yolk mixture and stir well.

6. Choose two half-slices of bread to put on her plate. Spread one piece of bread with the egg salad and top it with the other piece of bread.

Talk About
• Why does an egg have a shell? What does the shell do for the egg? The shell protects the egg. What does *protect* mean?
• Who protects you? How does God protect you?
• Who protected the people in our story? What happened?

Suggested Bible Stories
Jacob's Dream
Baby Moses
Crossing the Red Sea
The Sun Stands Still
David and Goliath
Esther
The Fiery Furnace
Daniel and the Lions
Joseph, Mary, and Jesus Go to Egypt
Peter Escapes From Prison
Paul and Silas in Prison
Paul's Shipwreck

Color Cookies

Ingredients
roll of refrigerated sugar cookie dough
jelly beans or gum drops

Kitchen Tools
aluminum foil
baking sheet
oven
pot holders
paper towels

Prepare Ahead of Time
Preheat the oven to the temperature recommended on the package of dough. Slice the cookie dough.

Guide Each Child To
1. Get a piece of aluminum foil to work on.
2. Place a slice of cookie dough on the foil.
3. Choose a jelly bean or gum drop.
4. Push the jelly bean or gum drop into the center of his cookie dough.
5. Bake according to the time and temperature recommended on the package of dough.

Talk About
• What is your favorite color? Who made colors?
• What other things are the same color as your jelly bean or gum drop?
• What had lots of colors in our story? What happened?

Suggested Bible Stories
Creation of Light and Color
Noah
Joseph's Colorful Coat
John Sees Heaven

Peanut Butter

Ingredients
a few peanuts in the shell
2 cups roasted peanuts
½ teaspoon salt
1 tablespoon peanut oil
crackers

Kitchen Tools
blender
paper plates
mixing bowl, spoon
paper towels
plastic knives
measuring cups, spoons

Guide Each Child To
1. Examine the peanuts in the shell and crack one open to see inside.
2. Help grind the peanuts in the blender, ½ cup at a time.
3. Put the ground peanuts in a bowl.
4. Stir in peanut oil and salt.
5. Put the peanut mixture back into the blender one cup at a time, adding a few drops of oil if necessary.
6. Blend the peanut mixture until smooth.
7. Spread the peanut butter on crackers.

Talk About
• What covers the peanut while it's growing under the ground? (The shell protects the peanut.) How does the shell protect it?
• What does *protect* mean? Who protects you or takes care of you?
• Who protected the person in our story? What happened?

Suggested Bible Stories
Noah
Joseph Is Taken to Egypt
Baby Moses
Rahab and the Spies
David and Goliath
Esther
The Fiery Furnace
Daniel and the Lions
Jonah
The Lost Sheep
Paul in a Basket
Paul's Nephew Hears a Plot
Paul's Shipwreck

Silver Dollar Pancakes

Ingredients (for 100 pancakes)
2 cups flour
1 teaspoon salt
1 teaspoon baking soda
2 tablespoons sugar
2 eggs, slightly beaten
2 cups buttermilk
2 tablespoons melted margarine
cooking spray
butter and syrup, if you wish

Kitchen Tools
mixing bowl, spoon, pancake turner
skillet or griddle
paper plates
measuring cups, spoons
plastic forks, knives
paper towels

Prepare Ahead of Time
Bring a silver dollar if you can, or bring quarters.
Melt the butter. Heat the skillet to 350 degrees.

Guide Each Child To
1. Help stir the flour, baking soda, salt, and sugar together in the mixing bowl.
2. Add buttermilk, eggs, and melted butter. Stir well.
3. Spray the skillet with cooking spray.
4. Spoon the batter onto the skillet by teaspoons to make pancakes the size of a silver dollar.
5. Watch for bubbles to appear on the top and edges of the pancakes, and turn the pancakes over when bubbles appear.
6. Serve the pancakes onto paper plates.

Talk About
• Have you ever seen a silver dollar? (Bring some coins if you want.)
• Which will buy more—a quarter or a silver dollar? Have you ever bought anything with money of your own? How did you get your money?
• Who do we thank for our money? Why? How does God want us to use our money?
• Who used money in our story? What happened?

Suggested Bible Stories
Joseph's Brothers Go to Egypt
Hidden Treasure
The Pearl of Great Price
The Lost Coin
The Widow's Mite
Tax Money in a Fish

Tuna Salad

Ingredients
1 can of tuna
apple
dill or sweet pickles
mayonnaise
boiled egg
crackers

Kitchen Tools
knife
spoon, fork
can opener
bowl
paper towels

Prepare Ahead of Time
Boil the egg(s).

Guide Each Child To
1. Let the teacher open the tuna can.
2. Let the teacher cut the apple, pickles, and egg into small pieces.
3. Taste some of each ingredient. (You might want them to close their eyes and guess what they're eating.)
4. Help mix all the ingredients in a bowl.
5. Help the teacher add enough mayonnaise to moisten the mixture.
6. Put some tuna salad on a cracker.

Talk About
• How does the pickle taste? How does the apple taste? Does the egg taste like the apple? Does the tuna taste the same or different?
• The way things taste is called their flavor. Who made flavors? Who made mouths and tongues?
• Who tasted some flavors in our story? What happened?

Suggested Bible Stories
Creation of People
Adam and Eve Eat the Fruit
Abraham and the Three Visitors
Birthright and Blessing
Manna and Quail
Twelve Spies
Ravens Feed Elijah
A Widow Shares With Elijah
Daniel Refuses the Kings Food
John the Baptist
Birds and Flowers (Sermon on the Mount)
Jesus Feeds 5,000
Mary and Martha

Pita Pocket Message

Ingredients
pita bread

Kitchen Tools
knife
plastic sandwich bags

Prepare Ahead of Time
Write the promise verses on slips of paper.

Guide Each Child To
1. Put her slip of paper into a sandwich bag.
2. Let the teacher cut each pita in half to make two pockets.
3. Slip her sandwich bag into a pita half.

Talk About
- What does the verse say? What does it mean?
- Who said it?
- Why is it important?

Promise Verses
Joshua 1:15; Psalm 25:12; Psalm 32:7, 8; Psalm 34:18, 22; Psalm 37:5, 6, 11; Psalm 37:18, 19; Psalm 37:23, 24; Psalm 37:27, 28; Psalm 41:1-3; Psalm 50:15; Psalm 55:22; Isaiah 1:18; Isaiah 41:10, 13; Isaiah 46:4; Isaiah 58:9; Isaiah 60:20; Isaiah 58:11; Isaiah 65:17; Matthew 7:7; Matthew 11:28, 29; Matthew 28:20; Mark 10:27; John 8:32; John 11:25; John 14:12; John 14:14; John 14:27; John 16:13; John 16:24; Acts 1:11

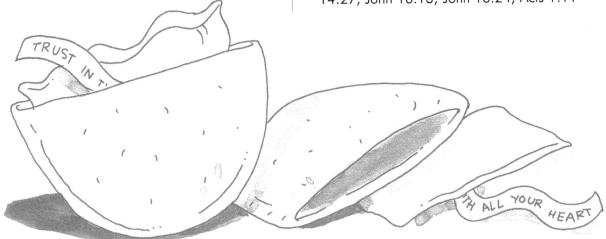

Cracker Fish in Soup

Ingredients
can of beef consommé or tomato soup
water
fish-shaped crackers

Kitchen Tools
pot
hot plate or stove
spoon
Styrofoam cups
paper towels
plastic spoons

Prepare Ahead of Time
Heat soup until it is just warm enough for the children.

Guide Each Child To
1. Put several "fish" into his soup.
2. Eat soup and crackers.

Talk About
• Where do fish live? What else lives in water? What are some different kinds of fish you can think of?
• Who made fish? Who made lakes and seas?
• What happened with fish in our story?

Suggested Bible Stories
Creation of Animals
Jonah
Jesus Chooses Twelve Friends
The Great Catch of Fish
The Fish and the Net
Jesus Feeds 5,000
Tax Money in a Fish
Jesus Makes Breakfast for His Friends

Peanut Butter Delight

Ingredients (for about 2 cups)
1 cup milk
2 teaspoons peanut butter
¼ teaspoon honey
¼ teaspoon vanilla
4 to 6 ice cubes
1 teaspoon sugar (optional)

Kitchen Tools
blender
measuring spoons, cups
paper cups
paper towels

Guide Each Child To
1. Help add the ingredients to the blender.
2. Let the teacher pour a small amount into a cup. Taste the drink.

Talk About
• We are mixing together some of God's gifts. What are they?
• Where does milk come from? Where does peanut butter come from? Where does honey come from? Where does vanilla come from?
• Would a person who is blind be able to enjoy this drink, even if he couldn't see it? Why? Could he tell what it was made of? How?
• Who was blind in our story? What happened?

Suggested Bible Stories
Isaac Gets a Wife
Jacob and Esau
Elisha's Room on the Roof
The Wise Men
Jesus Heals a Blind Man With Mud
Blind Bartimaeus
Perfume on Jesus' Feet
Paul to Damascus

Apricot Tea

Ingredients

one 18-ounce jar orange breakfast drink mix
¼ cup sugar
½ cup presweetened lemonade mix
½ cup instant decaffeinated tea
one 3-ounce package apricot gelatin
2½ teaspoons cinnamon
½ teaspoon ground cloves

Kitchen Tools

mixing bowl, spoon
measuring cups, spoons
warm to hot water (in kettle or thermos)
Styrofoam cups
paper towels

Guide Each Child To

1. Takes a turn helping mix the ingredients.
2. Help the teacher mix 1½ to 2 tablespoons of mix into 1 cup of hot water to serve one cup of tea.

Talk About

• What kinds of food are the best for making a healthy body? Which are your favorite? Who planned for us to eat good foods?
• What does it mean to share? How can you share your food?
• What are some reasons for giving to others? How does it feel when someone gives or shares with you?
• Who shared or gave in our story? What happened?

Suggested Bible Stories

Abraham and the Three Visitors
Ruth
David and Jonathan
A Widow Shares With Elijah
Elisha's Room on the Roof
Jesus Feeds 5,000
Mary and Martha

English Muffin Pizza

Ingredients
English muffins
sliced black olives
pepperoni
grated cheese
pizza sauce
mushrooms

Kitchen Tools
cookie sheet
broiler oven
pot holder
plastic spoons, knives
paper towels

Guide Each Child To
1. Spread sauce on one half of an English muffin.
2. Make a face on the pizza using the toppings.
(Olives can be eyes, pepperoni can be a mouth,
cheese can be hair, and so on.)
3. Let the teacher cook the pizza in the broiler
oven until the sauce bubbles or the cheese melts.

Talk About
• How are you special? (Not only because of
how you look, but also because of things you
can do.)
• How was the person in the story special?
What happened to him?

Suggested Bible Stories
Jacob and Esau
Samson
David Is Anointed
John the Baptist
Jesus and the Children
Zacchaeus

Candlesticks

Ingredients
half of 1 banana for each child
whipped cream
maraschino cherries (1 for each child)

Kitchen Tools
plastic spoons
paper plates
paper towels
knife to slice the bananas

Guide Each Child To
1. Let the teacher cut each banana in half.
2. Stand his half vertically on a plate. (You may need to cut both ends of each banana half in order to balance the banana so it will stand.)
3. Spoon a small bit of whipped cream onto the top end of the banana.
4. Place a cherry on top of the whipped cream. The banana is the candle and the cherry is the flame.

Talk About
• Who made light? Why do we need light?
• How do you get light in the daytime? How do you get light at night?
• Who saw light in our story? What happened?

Suggested Bible Stories
Creation of Light and Color
God Leads Israel With a Pillar of Fire
Gideon
Let Your Light Shine
The Lost Coin
John Sees Heaven

Floating Cloud

Ingredients (for 4 cups)
⅓ cup dry cocoa
⅓ cup sugar
⅛ teaspoon cinnamon
½ cup water
4 cups milk
¼ teaspoon vanilla
non-dairy whipped topping or a can
   of whipped cream

Kitchen Tools
cooking pot
Styrofoam cups
large spoon
stove or hot plate
measuring cups, spoons
paper towels

Guide Each Child To
1. Help mix the cocoa, sugar, cinnamon, and water in a pot.
2. Let the teacher stir the mixture constantly until it boils, then continue stirring for 1 minute.
3. Let the teacher stir in milk and heat to boiling again.
4. Help add vanilla and stir well.
5. Let the teacher pour the hot chocolate into cups.
6. Put a scoop of whipped cream onto her cup of hot chocolate. The whipped cream is the "cloud."

Talk About
• Whipped cream floats on the hot chocolate. Where does a cloud float?
• What is a cloud? Who made clouds? Tell about the cloud in the story.

Suggested Bible Stories
Creation of Sky, Sea, and Land
Crossing the Red Sea
Elijah on Mt. Carmel
Jesus Goes Back to Heaven

Pine-Orange Whip

Ingredients (for 1 child)
¼ cup cold pineapple juice
¼ cup cold orange juice
¼ cup cold skim milk
4 crushed ice cubes

Kitchen Tools
measuring cups
blender
cups

Prepare Ahead of Time
Multiply the measurements for the drink ingredients by the number of drinks you will need.

Guide Each Child To
1. Help the teacher pour the ingredients into the blender.
2. Add ice cubes to the mixture.
3. Let the teacher blend the mixture until bubbly.

Talk About
• Talk about cooperation as the children make the drink: one child adding something, one stirring, one measuring, and so on.
• Can you think of some things that are better done alone? What are some things that you have to do with others? How did God plan for friends to act toward each other?
• Did the people in the story cooperate or not? What happened?

Suggested Bible Stories
Tower of Babel
Abraham and Lot
David and Jonathan
A Widow's Oil Jars
Rebuilding Jerusalem's Walls
Daniel Refuses the King's Food
Jesus Chooses Twelve Friends
Through the Roof
The Good Samaritan
Timothy
Paul and Silas in Prison

Sunshine Muffins

Ingredients
English muffins
processed American cheese slices

Kitchen Tools
knife
cookie sheet
oven or broiler
pot holder
paper towels
oven mitt

Prepare Ahead of Time
Cut the cheese slices in sunshine shapes as shown. For fastest cutting, stack them and cut them all at once. If you are using an oven, preheat it to 350 degrees.

Guide Each Child To
1. Choose a "sunshine" of cheese and half of an English muffin.
2. Place the cheese slice on the muffin.
3. Give the sunshine muffin to an adult to put in the oven or under the broiler.

Talk About
• What happens to the night as soon as the sun starts coming up?
• Who made the sun?
• What was the light in our story? What happened?

Suggested Bible Stories
Creation of Sun, Moon, and Stars
Joseph's Dreams
The Sun Stands Still
Jesus Is Born
John Sees Heaven

Toasty Peanut Sticks

Ingredients (for 40 sticks)
9 slices of bread
1 cup of peanut butter
½ teaspoon salt
¼ cup oil

Kitchen Tools
knife
measuring spoons
bowl
plastic bag
mixing spoon
paper towels

Prepare Ahead of Time
Cut the crust off the slices. Save the crusts. Cut each slice into five sticks. Toast the crusts and bread at 250 degrees for 40 minutes.

Guide Each Child To
1. Put all of the crusts and five of the breadsticks into the plastic bag.
2. Crush the crusts and five sticks into small crumbs.
3. Help mix peanut butter, salt, and oil in the bowl.
4. Dip the remaining breadsticks into the mixture and then roll them in the crumbs.

Talk About
• Who had bread in our story? Do we know what kind of bread they had?
• When Jesus said, "Give us this day our daily bread," what did he mean?
• What should we tell God when he has blessed us with food to eat? How can we thank him?

Suggested Bible Stories
Abraham and the Three Visitors
Manna and Quail
A Widow Shares With Elijah
Jesus Feeds 5,000
The Lord's Prayer
The Lord's Supper

Crunchy Chewies

Ingredients
1 cup peanut butter
1 cup instant dry milk
½ cup honey
crisp rice cereal

Kitchen Tools
measuring cups
mixing spoon
paper towels
waxed paper

Guide Each Child To
1. Help measure and mix the peanut butter, instant milk, and honey.
2. Roll a heaping teaspoonful of the mixture into a ball on waxed paper.
3. Roll the ball in the crisp rice cereal.

Talk About
• How did you obey? What would happen to our recipe if you didn't follow it?
• Why must we obey our parents?
• Who obeyed in our story?

Suggested Bible Stories
Adam and Eve Eat the Fruit
Abraham Travels
Joseph in Prison
Joseph Leads Egypt
Crossing the Red Sea (Moses leads the Israelites)
The Ten Commandments
Balaam's Talking Donkey
Naaman
King Josiah Finds God's Word
The Wise Man's House
Two Sons and a Vineyard

Treasure Cookies

Ingredients (for about 15 cookies)
¾ cup margarine
1 tablespoon vanilla
¼ cup plus 2 tablespoons sugar
1¼ cups plus 2 tablespoons flour
gum drops or jelly beans

Kitchen Tools

bowl	pot holder
refrigerator	oven
electric mixer	paper towels
spatula	cookie sheet
measuring cups, spoon	

Prepare Ahead of Time
Beat margarine, sugar, and vanilla until light and fluffy. Add the flour. Beat at a low speed until well blended. Refrigerate for at least 1 hour.

Guide Each Child To
1. Pat a tablespoon of dough into a thick circle.
2. Place a jelly bean or gum drop in the center of the dough circle.
3. Bring the sides of the dough up and over the jelly bean or gum drop, rolling the dough into a ball with a "treasure" inside.
4. Let the teacher bake the treasure cookies at 375 degrees for 8 to 10 minutes.
5. Wait for the cookies to cool before eating.

Talk About
• What was hidden in the story? Who found it?
• What kind of treasure does God want us to have?
• What was the treasure in the story? What happened?

Suggested Bible Stories
King Josiah Finds God's Word
Tax Money in a Fish
Hidden Treasure
The Lost Coin

Edible Map

Ingredients and Materials
crescent roll dough
flour
U.S. map or globe
pictures of different land forms (islands, volcanoes, mountains, caves)

Kitchen Tools
foil
waxed paper
cookie sheet
oven
pot holder
paper towels

Guide Each Child To
1. Look at the map or globe and the pictures.
2. Discuss the characteristics of the land forms.
3. On the foil, mold a portion of the dough into a land form of his choice. (The foil represents water.)
4. Add flour as needed to keep the dough from becoming too sticky.
5. Let the teacher bake the "land forms" according to the directions on the dough package.

Talk About
• How is a seashore different from mountains? Have you ever seen any of these land forms?
• What is the land like where you live? Who made the different land forms? How?

Suggested Bible Stories
Creation of Sky, Sea, and Land
Abraham and Lot
Twelve Spies
Israelites Wander in the Wilderness
Paul's Shipwreck

NOTE: This is also a good activity for the study of missions and missionaries.

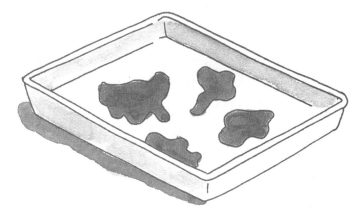

Fish Dinner

Ingredients
fish sticks

Kitchen Tools
cookie sheet
foil
oven
pot holder
paper towels

Prepare Ahead of Time
Preheat the oven according to the package instructions.

Guide Each Child To
1. Help place fish sticks on the pan.
2. Let the teacher bake the fish sticks according to the package instructions.
3. Choose one or two fish sticks to eat.

Talk About
- Who made fish? Where do fish live?
- What other water creatures can you name?
- What water creatures were in our story? What happened?

Suggested Bible Stories
Creation of Animals
Jonah
Jesus Chooses Twelve Friends
The Great Catch of Fish
The Fish and the Net
Jesus Feeds 5,000
Tax Money in a Fish
Jesus Makes Breakfast for His Friends

Mangers

Ingredients
2 bags of butterscotch chips
1 can chow mein noodles
1 can cocktail peanuts
1 bag small pretzel twists

Kitchen Tools
sauce pan
stirring spoon
stove or hot plate
paper plates
plastic spoons
paper towels

Prepare Ahead of Time
Find or draw a picture of a manger.

Guide Each Child To
1. Help the teacher melt butterscotch chips in a saucepan.
2. Stir in peanuts and chow mein noodles.
3. Let the teacher place a spoonful of the mixture onto his paper plate.
4. Press his plastic spoon down into the center of the mixture to make it look like a manger.
5. Gently press a pretzel twist onto each end of the manger. (Do this before the mixture cools. The pretzels form the manger legs.)
6. Look at the picture of the manger.

Talk About
• Why did Joseph and Mary have to stay in a stable? Why did Mary put baby Jesus in a manger?
• Who came to see the baby? How did they know about him?
• Who was baby Jesus?

Suggested Bible Story
Jesus Is Born

121

Noodle Nibbles

Ingredients
one 3-ounce can of chow mein noodles
3 tablespoons melted margarine
2 teaspoons soy sauce
¼ teaspoon celery salt
dash of onion powder

Kitchen Tools
measuring spoons
oven
sauce pan
pot holder
large plastic container with lid
paper towels
cookie sheet

Prepare Ahead of Time
Preheat the oven to 275 degrees. Melt the margarine.

Guide Each Child To
1. Help measure and combine the margarine and soy sauce.
2. Pour the mixture over the chow mein noodles in the plastic container.
3. Toss the noodles in the container until they are coated with the sauce.
4. Sprinkle with celery salt and a dash of onion powder.
5. Close the lid and toss the noodles again.
6. Pour noodles onto the baking sheet.
7. Let the teacher bake the noodles for 12 to 15 minutes at 275 degrees.

Talk About
• How are you helping us make our snack?
• How do you help at home? How do you help in our classroom?
• Who helped in our story? How did they help?

Suggested Bible Stories
Jacob and Rachel
Moses and Aaron Before Pharaoh
Rahab and the Spies
Ruth
Saul Looks for Lost Donkeys
David, the Shepherd Boy
A Widow's Oil Jars
An Ax Head Floats
Jesus Chooses Twelve Friends
Through the Roof
Mary and Martha
Jesus Washes His Friends' Feet

Fruit Harvest Pizza

Ingredients
refrigerated sugar cookie dough
cooking oil spray
fresh fruit slices

Kitchen Tools
knife
pot holder
pizza pan
spatula
oven
paper towels

Prepare Ahead of Time
Preheat the oven according to package instructions. Slice the fresh fruit. Lightly spray the pizza pan with cooking oil.

Guide Each Child To
1. Help shape a pizza crust out of cookie dough on the pizza pan.
2. Let the teacher bake the dough according to package instructions.
3. Spread slices of fresh fruit over the cookie pizza.
4. Let the teacher slice the pizza and serve.

Talk About
• What kind of fruit is your favorite?
• Who gives us food to eat?
• What kind of food did the people in our story eat? Do you think you would have liked that food?

Suggested Bible Stories
Creation of Plants
Adam and Eve Eat the Fruit
Abraham and the Three Visitors
Birthright and Blessing
Manna and Quail
Ravens Feed Elijah
A Widow Shares With Elijah
Daniel Refuses the King's Food
Jesus Feeds 5,000
Mary and Martha
The Lord's Supper
Jesus Makes Breakfast for His Friends

Peach Sherbet

Ingredients
½ cup nonfat sour cream
2 tablespoon plus 2 teaspoons sugar
2 teaspoons lemon juice
1 teaspoon vanilla
15 ounces frozen peaches

Kitchen Tools
small bowl
small paper cups
mixing spoon
plastic spoons
measuring cups, spoons
paper towels
blender

Guide Each Child To
1. Help mix the sour cream, sugar, lemon juice, and vanilla in the small bowl.
2. Crush the frozen peaches in the blender.
3. Add the sour cream mixture to the peaches and blend again.
4. Dip some of the sherbet into her cup.
5. Say a thank-you prayer to God before eating.

Talk About
• What is prayer? Where can we pray?
• Why do we pray before we eat? When are some other times we can pray?
• Who prayed in our story? What happened?

Suggested Bible Stories
Isaac Gets a Wife
Hannah Prays for a Baby
David Plays the Harp
Daniel and the Lions
The Lord's Prayer
A Pharisee and a Tax Collector Pray
Paul and Silas in Prison

Honey Cookies

Ingredients (for about 4 dozen)

2 cups sugar   ½ teaspoon salt
1 egg   2 cups flour
1 stick margarine   2 teaspoons baking
2 tablespoons honey   powder

Kitchen Tools

two mixing bowls   measuring cups, spoons
oven   spatula
mixing spoon   cookie sheet
pot holder   paper towels

Prepare Ahead of Time

Preheat oven to 350 degrees.
NOTE: Have an extra, small amount of each ingredient ready for the first part of the activity.

Guide Each Child To

1. Take a turn mixing small amounts of each ingredient, without instruction or recipe.
2. Let the teacher bake their "recipe."
3. Listen to a leader read the recipe, and follow his instructions as he reads.
4. Mix the ingredients according to the leader's instructions.
5. Roll the dough into 1-inch balls and place them on the cookie sheet.
6. Let the teacher bake the cookies at 350 degrees for 8 minutes.

Talk About

• Did the two batches of cookies turn out differently? How?
• What was it like to make cookies without a leader? Did they taste good?
• Did you like one cookie better than the other? Which one? Why do you think it is better?
• Who was the leader in our story? What happened?

Suggested Bible Stories

Joseph Leads Egypt
Crossing the Red Sea (Moses leads the Israelites)
The Sun Stands Still
Deborah
Gideon
David Is Anointed
Solomon's Dream
Elijah on Mt. Carmel
Singers Lead Jehoshaphat's Army
Rebuilding Jerusalem's Walls (Nehemiah leads)
Esther

Hot Cider

Ingredients
1 quart of apple juice
3 cloves
1 quart of cranberry juice
¼ teaspoon allspice
2 tablespoons lemon juice
¼ teaspoon nutmeg
1 stick cinnamon

Kitchen Tools
large pot
stirring spoon
stove or hot plate
Styrofoam cups
strainer
paper towels
measuring cups, spoons

Guide Each Child To
1. Help put the ingredients in the large pot.
2. Wait for the mixture to heat to a boil. Watch the teacher strain out the spices, and pour cider for each child.

Talk About
• Discuss waiting. We have to wait for many things like Christmas, birthdays, and vacations.
• Who was waiting in our story? What happened?

Suggested Bible Stories
Isaac Is Born
The Plagues in Egypt
Israelites Wander in the Wilderness
Jericho's Walls Fall Down
Samuel Hears God
Elijah on Mt. Carmel
Jonah
John the Baptist Is Born
Anna and Simeon
The Resurrection
Peter Escapes From Prison

Health Muffins

Ingredients (for about 2 dozen)

½ cup boiling water
1 cup wheat germ
1 cup bran flakes
2 cups buttermilk
½ cup cooking oil
2½ cups flour

1 cup oats
2½ teaspoons soda
½ pound brown sugar
½ teaspoon salt
2 eggs, beaten

Kitchen Tools

greased muffin tins (or use baking cup liners)
oven
measuring cups, spoons
pot holder
mixing bowl
paper towels
mixing spoon

Prepare Ahead of Time

Preheat oven to 400 degrees.

Boil water. Pour the ½ cup boiling water over the cereal to let it soften. WARNING: Do not allow the children to get near the boiling water.

Guide Each Child To

1. Help measure the ingredients and mix them into the softened bran cereal.
2. Stir the batter.
3. Spoon the batter into the muffin tins.
4. Let the teacher bake the muffins for 15 to 20 minutes at 400 degrees.

Talk About

• What happens if you don't follow the recipe? What if you put in ½ pound of salt instead of brown sugar?
• Why is it important to follow directions and obey them?
• Who followed instructions and obeyed in our story? What happened?

Suggested Bible Stories

Adam and Eve Eat the Fruit
The Ten Commandments
Naaman
King Josiah Finds God's Word
Jonah
Jesus Is Tempted
The Wise Man's House
Two Sons and a Vineyard

Double Thumbprint Cookies

Ingredients (for about 30 cookies)

¾ cup sugar

2 eggs

1 teaspoon vanilla

1 cup chocolate chips

2 cups of oats

1½ cups of flour

1 teaspoon baking powder

¼ teaspoon salt

peanut butter

Kitchen Tools

electric mixer

paper towels

mixing bowl, spoon

oven

smaller bowl

baking sheet

measuring cups, spoons

pot holders

paper plates, plastic spoons

Prepare Ahead of Time

Preheat the oven to 350 degrees.

Guide Each Child To

1. Choose one partner to work with.
2. Help beat the sugar, eggs, and vanilla.
3. Help melt the chocolate chips in the smaller bowl in a microwave or oven. Add the melted chips to the sugar mixture.
4. Stir in the oats, flour, baking powder, and salt.
5. Roll a 1-inch ball of dough for himself, while his partner makes a ball of dough.

6. Place the dough on a baking sheet. Gently press his thumb into the center of his cookie ball, then into the center of his friend's cookie ball. His partner does the same with his cookie, so that each cookie has two thumbprints.
7. Spoon peanut butter into the thumbprint on his cookie.
8. Bake at 350 degrees for 10 to 12 minutes.

Talk About

• How did your friend help you? How did you help your friend?

• Who planned for us to have friends? Who are some of your friends? What is a good friend like?

• Who were the friends in our story? What happened?

Suggested Bible Stories

Creation of People (God makes Eve)

Samson

David and Jonathan

The Fiery Furnace

Jesus Chooses Twelve Friends

Jesus and the Children

Rapid Rise Rolls

Ingredients (for about 3 dozen)

1 package rapid-rise yeast
4½ cups flour
4 teaspoons baking powder
½ teaspoon soda
1 teaspoon salt
¼ cup sugar
1½ cups buttermilk
¼ cup oil

Kitchen Tools

sauce pan
knife
mixing bowl
clean dish towel
stirring spoon

oven and stove top
measuring cups, spoons
pot holder
paper towels

Prepare Ahead of Time

Preheat the oven to 400 degrees.

Guide Each Child To

1. Take a good look at the yeast and smell it. Listen as the teacher explains that the yeast will make the rolls big and puffy.
2. Help measure and mix the yeast, flour, baking powder, soda, salt, and sugar.
3. Let the teacher scald the buttermilk and oil (120 to 130 degrees, when tiny bubbles form around the edges of the pan).
4. Let the teacher add the liquid to the mixture.
5. Help knead the dough, lightly.
6. Help roll out the dough to ⅜ inches thick.
7. Cut out rolls and let rise for 30 minutes. Observe the rolls before and after rising.
8. Let the teacher bake the rolls for 15 minutes at 400 degrees.

Talk About

• What does the yeast do to the dough? (It makes it big and puffy. It helps the dough rise.)
• How did you help to make the rolls?
• How do you help at home? How do you help in class?

Suggested Bible Stories

Jacob and Rachel
Baby Moses (Miriam watches and helps)
Moses and Aaron Before Pharaoh
Ruth
David, the Shepherd Boy
A Widow Shares With Elijah
A Widow's Oil Jars
An Ax Head Floats
Jesus Chooses Twelve Friends
Through the Roof
Philip and the Man From Ethiopia
Dorcas

Pigs in a Blanket

Ingredients

hot dogs, 1 for every two children
canned, refrigerated crescent roll dough
American or mild cheddar cheese

Kitchen Tools

knife for teacher's use
baking sheet
paper plates
oven
paper towels
pot holders

Prepare Ahead of Time

Cut each hot dog in half crosswise. Slice the cheese into thin sections about as long as the sliced hot dogs.

Preheat the oven to the temperature recommended on the package of dough.

Guide Each Child To

1. Put a triangle of crescent roll dough, a hot dog half, and a slice of cheese on his plate.
2. Put the hot dog on top of the dough.
3. Put the cheese on top of the hot dog.
4. Roll the edges of the dough around the hot dog and cheese and pinch them closed.
5. Let the teacher bake the "pigs in a blanket" according to the dough package instructions.

Talk About

• We call this snack "pigs in a blanket." What is the pig? What is the blanket?
• Do you have a blanket at home? When do you use it?
• Who takes care of you at night?
• Who was sleeping in our story? What happened? Was God with them?

Suggested Bible Stories

Jacob's Dream
Joseph's Dreams
Pharaoh's Dreams
Samson
Samuel Hears God
Solomon's Dream
Daniel and the Lions
The Wise Men (dream about Herod)
Jesus Stills the Storm
Peter and Cornelius
Peter Escapes From Prison

Breadstick People

Ingredients
canned, refrigerated breadstick dough
(one breadstick per child)
flour

Kitchen Tools
aluminum foil
oven
plastic knives
pot holders
baking sheet

Prepare Ahead of Time
Preheat the oven to the temperature recommended on the package of dough.

Guide Each Child To
1. Choose a piece of foil to work on and get a breadstick.
2. Sprinkle the breadstick with flour to keep it from getting too sticky.
3. Cut the stick into sections as shown to make legs, body, arms, and head.
4. Arrange the sections to make a person and pinch the sections together.
5. Bake on the foil according to package directions.

Talk About
• Who made people? Who were the people in our story?
• What was different about the person in our story? Did God (Jesus) love them anyway? What happened?
• How does God want us to treat people who may be different than we are? Why?
• How does God feel about you?

Suggested Bible Stories
Creation of People
David Is Anointed
David and Mephibosheth
John the Baptist
Through the Roof
The Man's Withered Hand
Woman Touches Jesus' Hem
Jesus Heals the Bent Woman
Ten Lepers
Jesus and the Children
Zacchaeus
Blind Bartimaeus
Peter and John Heal a Lame Man
Peter and Cornelius

1.  cut off ¼ dough

2. roll the ¼ piece to make arms

3.  cut here to make legs

Cinnamon Stars

Ingredients

canned, refrigerated Danish roll dough
 (1 roll for each child)
colored sugar sprinkles for cake decoration
flour

Kitchen Tools

waxed paper
pot holders
plastic knives
paper plates
oven
paper towels
baking sheet

Prepare Ahead of Time

Preheat the oven to the temperature recommended on package of dough.

Guide Each Child To

1. Choose a dough roll and a section of waxed paper (at least 12 inches long).
2. Unroll the dough to its full length.
3. Cut the long piece of dough in half.
4. Form each half into a triangle. (Flour on her hands can keep the dough from getting sticky.)
5. Put one triangle on top of the other to make a star of David. (See the illustration.)
6. Bake the dough according to package instructions.
7. Frost the star with the frosting found in the package of dough.
8. Sprinkle colored sugar on the star.

Talk About

• Who made stars? What do you like about stars?
• When do we see stars? Where are stars in the daytime?
• Who did we talk about in our story? Who took care of him at night? Who takes care of you at night?

Suggested Bible Stories

God's Promise to Abraham
Jacob's Dream
Joseph's Dreams
The Plagues in Egypt
God Leads Israel With a Pillar of Fire
Samuel Hears God
Solomon's Dream
Angels Appear to the Shepherds
The Wise Men
Nicodemus Visits Jesus at Night
Paul in a Basket
Peter Escapes From Prison
Paul's Nephew Hears a Plot

Apple Cinnamon Muffins

Ingredients (for 12 muffins)

1½ cups flour
½ cup wheat germ
¼ cup sugar
1 tablespoon baking powder
½ teaspoon salt
1 teaspoon cinnamon
1 cup chopped apple
1 cup milk
3 tablespoons vegetable oil
2 egg whites, lightly beaten
1 tablespoon sugar with ¼ teaspoon cinnamon

Kitchen Tools

two mixing bowls
muffin tins
mixing spoons
oven
measuring spoons, cups

pot holders
knife for teacher's use
paper plates,
paper towels
cooking spray

Prepare Ahead of Time

Preheat the oven to 400 degrees.

Guide Each Child To

1. Help mix the flour, wheat germ, ¼ cup sugar, baking powder, salt, and 1 teaspoon cinnamon in a bowl.
2. Watch and help as the teacher chops the apples to make 1 cup.
3. Help mix the milk, vegetable oil, egg whites, and apple in another bowl.
4. Add the apple mixture to flour mixture and stir.
5. Pour the batter into a muffin cup.
6. Help mix 1 tablespoon sugar and ¼ teaspoon cinnamon. Sprinkle the mixture on his muffin.
7. Bake 20 minutes at 400 degrees.

Talk About

- Who made sugar and salt and apples?
- What is your favorite food that God made?
- What food did the people in our story have? What happened?

Suggested Bible Stories

Birthright and Blessing
Manna and Quail
Ravens Feed Elijah
Daniel Refuses the King's Food
John the Baptist (locust and honey)
The Lord's Supper

Banana Muffins

Ingredients (for 12 muffins)
⅔ cup white flour
⅔ cup whole wheat flour
⅓ cup sugar
2 teaspoons baking powder
¾ cup buttermilk
1 egg
2 tablespoons margarine
¼ teaspoon lemon juice
2 ripe bananas
cooking spray

Kitchen Tools
two mixing bowls
oven
mixing spoons
pot holders
measuring cups, spoons

paper plates
fork to mash bananas
paper towels
muffin tins

Prepare Ahead of Time
Preheat the oven to 375 degrees.

Guide Each Child To
1. Help mix the flours, sugar, and baking powder in one bowl.
2. Help mix the buttermilk, egg, margarine, and lemon juice in another bowl.
3. Add the buttermilk mixture to the flour mixture and stir.
4. Mash bananas on a paper plate and add them to the mixture.
5. Spray the muffin tins with cooking spray.
6. Pour batter into a muffin cup in the muffin tin. Fill it three-fourths full.
7. Bake for 20 minutes at 375 degrees.

Talk About
• How did you help make the muffins? What job did you do?
• Why does God want us to help each other?
• Who helped in our story? What did that person do?
• How do you help at home? How do you help in class?

Suggested Bible Stories
Baby Moses (Miriam helps)
Rahab and the Spies
Ruth
A Widow's Oil Jars
Rebuilding Jerusalem's Walls
Jesus Chooses Twelve Friends
The Good Samaritan
Mary and Martha
Jesus Washes His Friends' Feet
Paul in a Basket
Dorcas

Mini Icees

Ingredients
ice
juice of your choice

Kitchen Tools
blender or ice crusher
long-handled mixing spoon
small paper cups (bathroom size)
plastic spoons
paper towels

Prepare Ahead of Time
Freeze the ice or get a bag of ice at the grocery store.

Guide Each Child To
1. Help put ice into the blender.
2. Help crush the ice in the blender.
3. Add juice a little at a time to keep the mixture thick and icy.
4. Put a scoop of the flavored crushed ice into her cup.

Talk About
• Sometimes ice comes down from the sky. What do we call it? (In warm weather, it's hail. In winter, it's sleet or snow.) Have you ever seen hail or sleet or snow? What was it like?
• Who made weather? What's your favorite weather? What was the weather like in our story?
• Who took care of the people in our story? Who takes care of you?

Suggested Bible Stories
Noah
The Plagues in Egypt (hail)
Jonah
Jesus Stills the Storm
Paul's Shipwreck

Dyed Eggs

Ingredients

eggs, at least 1 per child
food coloring
vinegar
water

Kitchen Tools

coffee cups or small bowls, one for each color of
    food coloring
tablespoon
spoons
paper towels
pot
stove

Prepare Ahead of Time

Boil the eggs.

Guide Each Child To

1. Help put water into the cups or bowls.
2. Help put a different color of food coloring into
each cup or bowl of water.
3. Help add 1 tablespoon vinegar to each cup or
bowl.
4. Dip his egg into the color he chooses to dye
his egg.
5. Let the egg sit in the colored water for 3 to 5
minutes. The longer the egg stays in the dye, the
darker it becomes.
6. Lift the egg out and let it dry on paper towels.

Talk About

• Who made colors?
• What was colorful in our story? What
happened?
• We are dipping eggs into water. Who
dipped into water in our story? Why? What
happened?
• Did you ever see anybody get baptized?
Why do people get baptized?

Suggested Bible Stories

Noah
Joseph's Colorful Coat
Naaman
Jesus Is Baptized
Philip and the Man From Ethiopia
Lydia
Peter and Cornelius
Paul and Silas in Prison

Cheese Fry Campfires

Ingredients
1 package of frozen, unseasoned french fries
8 to 10 ounces of cheddar or Colby cheese

Kitchen Tools
baking sheet
toaster oven or oven with broiler
aluminum foil
pot holders
cheese grater
paper plates
paper towels

Prepare Ahead of Time
Preheat the oven to the temperature recommended on the package of fries.

Describe a campfire to children. Tell them they will make small pretend campfires. They will pretend the fries are the logs and the cheese is the fire.

Guide Each Child To
1. Help cover the baking sheet with foil.
2. Choose five or six fries and stack them up like a campfire on the baking sheet.
3. Bake according to package directions.
4. Grate cheese on top of her fries.
5. Return the fries to the oven or place them under the broiler until the cheese melts and starts to bubble.

Talk About
• Have you ever gone camping? Have you ever seen a campfire? What was it like?
• Where was the fire in our story? What happened?

Suggested Bible Stories
Burning Bush
Gideon
David Spares Saul's Life at Night
Elijah on Mt. Carmel
The Fiery Furnace
Nicodemus Visits Jesus at Night
Jesus in Gethsemane
Jesus Makes Breakfast for His Friends
Paul on Malta

Gingerbread People

Ingredients (for about 2 dozen)
½ cup sugar
½ cup shortening
½ cup dark molasses
¼ cup water
2¾ cups flour plus extra flour
¾ teaspoon salt
¾ teaspoon ground ginger
½ teaspoon baking soda
¼ teaspoon cinnamon

Kitchen Tools
mixing bowl, spoon
oven
measuring cups, spoons
aluminum foil
baking sheet
electric mixer
pot holders
person-shaped cookie cutter
paper towels

Prepare Ahead of Time
Beat the sugar, shortening, molasses, and water in large bowl. Add flour, salt, ginger, baking soda, and cinnamon. Chill the dough in the refrigerator at least 1 hour. Preheat the oven to 375 degrees.

Guide Each Child To
1. Place some dough on a piece of aluminum foil.
2. Pat the dough flat, putting flour on his hands to keep the dough from getting too sticky.
3. Cut a figure out of the dough using the person-shaped cookie cutter.
4. Remove the excess dough. Shape it and flatten it to make a round cookie.
5. Place the foil with his cookie on it onto the baking sheet.
6. Let the teacher bake them at 375 degrees for 6 to 8 minutes.

Talk About
• Who made people?
• How are you like other people? How are you different?
• How was the person in the story special or different? Did God still love him? What happened?

Suggested Bible Stories
Twelve Spies (Joshua and Caleb)
Samson
Ruth
David and Mephibosheth
Naaman
John the Baptist
Jesus Chooses Twelve Friends
Through the Roof
Jesus Heals the Bent Woman
Ten Lepers
Zacchaeus

Cinnamon Toast

Ingredients
bread
soft margarine

cinnamon
sugar

Kitchen Tools
plastic knives
baking sheet
toaster oven or broiler
pot holder
paper plates

poster board
paper towels
marker

Prepare Ahead of Time
Make a rebus chart recipe on the poster board as shown.

Guide Each Child To
Follow the directions given on the rebus chart with as little help as possible.

Talk About
• What would happen if you didn't follow the directions? What if you sprinkled on salt instead of sugar? What if you didn't put margarine on the bread?
• What happens if we don't follow God's rules?
• Why does God have rules for us to obey?

Suggested Bible Stories
Adam and Eve Eat the Fruit
The Ten Commandments
Naaman
King Josiah Finds God's Law
Jonah
Jesus Is Tempted
The Wise Man's House
Two Sons and a Vineyard

Scroll Rolls

Ingredients
refrigerated crescent roll dough, enough for each
    child to get 2 rolls
flour

Kitchen Tools
baking sheet
oven
pot holders
paper plates
paper towels

Prepare Ahead of Time
Preheat the oven to the temperature recommended
on the package of dough.

Guide Each Child To
1. Separate the dough into rectangles, instead of
separating the dough into triangles at the perfora-
tions. (Each rectangle will contain two triangles.)
2. With the dough on her plate, roll up the two
short sides so that they meet in the center as shown.
3. Place the scroll roll dough onto the baking
sheet.
4. Let the teacher bake the rolls according to the
package instructions.

Talk About
- What is a scroll?
- What was written on the scroll in our story?
What happened?
- Where do we read God's words?

Suggested Bible Stories
King Josiah Finds God's Word
Jesus as a Boy in the Temple
Philip and the Man From Ethiopia

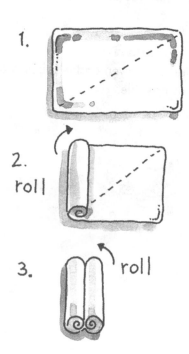

1.

2. roll

3. roll

Berry Bush Pies

Ingredients (for about 12)
2 cups flour
1¼ teaspoons salt
½ cup vegetable oil
5 tablespoons cold water
2 or 3 kinds of fresh or frozen berries

Kitchen Tools
large and small mixing bowls
oven
pot holders
measuring cups, spoons
paper plates, plastic spoons
mixing spoon
muffin pans
paper towels

Prepare Ahead of Time
Preheat the oven to 450 degrees.

Guide Each Child To
1. Help stir the flour and salt together in large bowl.
2. Pour the vegetable oil into small bowl. Add water, but don't stir.
3. Pour the liquid into the flour and salt mixture. Take turns stirring until the dough makes a ball.
4. Put a small amount of dough into a muffin cup, pressing it down and up the sides.
5. Bake the dough at 450 degrees for 10 minutes.
6. While the pie crusts are baking, mix berries in the large bowl.
7. Set his baked pie crust on his plate and spoon berries into it.

Talk About
• Everybody helped make our pies. Who helped in our story? How did they help?
• How do you help at home? How do you help in class?
• Why does God want us to help each other?

Suggested Bible Stories
Baby Moses (Miriam helps)
Rahab and the Spies
Ruth
A Widow's Oil Jars
An Ax Head Floats
The Good Samaritan
Jesus Washes His Friends' Feet

Fruit Punch

Ingredients
powdered, sweetened fruit punch mix
1½ cups lemon-lime soda
1 quart of water
1 pint of orange or lime sherbet (optional)

Kitchen Tools
pitcher
paper cups
long-handled spoon
plastic spoons
dry measuring cups, spoons
paper towels
liquid measuring cups

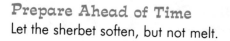

Prepare Ahead of Time
Let the sherbet soften, but not melt.

Guide Each Child To
1. Help put the water into the pitcher.
2. Help add the amount of powdered mix recommended on the package to make 1 quart of punch.
3. Take turns stirring the drink mix into the water.
4. Help add 1½ cups lemon-lime soda and stir.
5. Pour some of the punch into her cup.
6. Dip one small plastic spoonful of sherbet and add it to her cup of punch.

Talk About
• People sometimes have punch like this at parties. Did you ever go to a party? What was it like?
• What was the party in our story? Why did they have the party? What happened?

Suggested Bible Stories
Esther
Writing on the Wall
Water Into Wine
The Runaway Son

Cloud Gelatin

Ingredients
2½ cups boiling water
two 8-ounce packages of blue or purple gelatin mix
non-dairy whipped topping

Kitchen Tools
mixing bowl, spoon
scissors
pancake turner
13-by-9-inch pan
paper plates, plastic spoons
baking sheet
knife
paper towels
waxed paper

Prepare Ahead of Time
Mix the boiling water with the gelatin mix. Pour into the pan and refrigerate at least 3 hours. Dip the bottom of the pan into warm water for about 15 seconds.

Draw a 3-inch wide cloud onto waxed paper. Cut this out and use it as a pattern. Place the pattern on the gelatin and cut around it. Cut out one cloud for each child. Lift the gelatin cloud out of the pan and place it onto the baking sheet. Keep refrigerated until class time.

Guide Each Child To
1. Place a gelatin cloud on a paper plate.
2. Using his spoon, "frost" the cloud with the whipped topping.

Talk About
• Who made clouds?
• What are clouds like?
• Tell about the cloud in the story. What happened?

Suggested Bible Stories
Elijah on Mt. Carmel (servant sees a cloud)
Jesus Goes Back to Heaven
John Sees Heaven

Fruit Yogurt Sundaes

Ingredients
one 8-ounce container of vanilla yogurt
1 tablespoon of lemon or orange gelatin mix
1 can mandarin oranges
2 bananas
1 cup grapes
¼ teaspoon cinnamon

Kitchen Tools
large and small mixing bowls
knife
plastic bowls, spoons
can opener
mixing spoons
paper towels
measuring spoons

Prepare Ahead of Time
Open the can of mandarin oranges. Just before the activity, slice the bananas into a small plastic bowl.

Guide Each Child To
1. Help stir 1 tablespoon of gelatin mix into the yogurt in the small mixing bowl.
2. Help put the oranges, bananas, grapes, and cinnamon into the large mixing bowl. Take a turn stirring the fruit.
3. Put a big spoonful of fruit into his bowl.
4. Place a small spoonful of yogurt mixture on top.

Talk About
• What kind of fruit do you like best?
• Who made fruit?
• What kind of food did the people in our story eat? What happened?

Suggested Bible Stories
Adam and Eve Eat the Fruit
Abraham and the Three Visitors
Twelve Spies
John the Baptist (locusts and honey)
The Lord's Supper

Bloomin' Apple

Ingredients

apples, at least 1 for every four children
1 tablespoon brown sugar for each apple
1 teaspoon margarine for each apple
⅛ teaspoon cinnamon for each apple

Kitchen Tools

knife for teacher's use
baking pan
small bowl
measuring spoons
mixing spoons
plastic knives, forks
paper plates

Prepare Ahead of Time

Just before the activity, slice the apples from top to bottom so that you have at least two 2 per child.
    Melt the margarine.
    Preheat the oven to 350 degrees.

Guide Each Child To

1. Arrange her apple slices with other children's slices to look like flower petals on the baking pan as shown.
2. Help mix the brown sugar, melted margarine, and cinnamon.
3. Use a plastic knife to dot the sugar and cinnamon mixture on her apple slices.

4. Bake the apple slices at 350 degrees for 10 minutes.
5. Cool and eat.

Talk About
• Who made flowers? What are some other kinds of plants?
• What kind of tree does an apple come from? What other fruits grow on trees?
• What kind of plant was in our story? What happened?

Suggested Bible Stories

Creation of Plants
Adam and Eve Eat the Fruit
Burning Bush
Aaron's Staff Blooms
Birds and Flowers (Sermon on the Mount)
The Triumphal Entry
The Resurrection (garden tomb)

Rainbow Sandwiches

Ingredients
bread
cream cheese, softened
food coloring (four colors)

Kitchen Tools
small plastic bowls
spoons
plastic knives
sharp knife for teacher's use
paper plates
paper towels

Prepare Ahead of Time
Cut the crusts off of the bread.

Soften the cream cheese. Divide the cream cheese evenly among four bowls, one bowl for each color of food coloring.

Guide Each Child To
1. Help put food coloring in the bowls of cream cheese and take a turn stirring it until the color is blended in.
2. Spread one slice of bread with one color of cream cheese.
3. Stack his slice of bread on top of slices that other children have spread with the other three colors. (When each child does this, there will be several four-layer sandwiches.)
4. Let the teacher cut across each sandwich to make four square sandwiches.
5. Place his sandwich on his plate and eat it.

Talk About
- Where would we look to see a rainbow?
- Who makes rainbows? What are some of the colors in rainbows?
- What was colorful in our story? What happened?

Suggested Bible Stories
Noah
Joseph's Colorful Coat

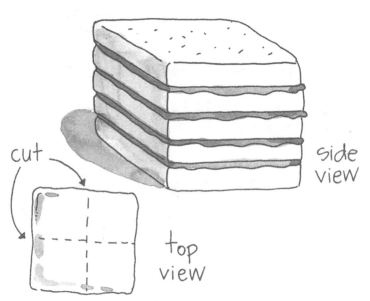

cut

side view

top view

Flower Cookies

Ingredients
1 roll of refrigerated sugar cookie dough
flour
food coloring

Kitchen Tools
knife for teacher's use
baking sheet
oven
pot holders
small, clean paintbrushes
paper cups
aluminum foil
paper towels

Prepare Ahead of Time
Wash and clean the paintbrushes.

Cut the aluminum foil into 4-inch squares so that you have one square for each child.

Slice the cookie dough into 30 round slices. Then cut each slice into fourths like a pie. Keep the dough chilled until ready to use.

Pour food coloring into paper cups, one cup for each color.

Guide Each Child To
1. Choose six pieces of cookie dough (six fourths).
2. Roll one fourth into a ball and place it in the middle of her piece of aluminum foil. (A little flour on the hands will help keep the dough from getting too sticky.)
3. Push her thumb gently into the ball of dough to flatten it a little.
4. Place the other five pieces of dough around the ball, points facing the ball as shown to make petals on a flower.
5. Paint her flower with food coloring and a paint-brush.
6. Bake according to package directions.

Talk About
- Who made flowers?
- What kind of flower is your favorite?
- Who was in a garden in our story? What happened?

Suggested Bible Stories
Creation of Plants
Garden of Eden
Aaron's Staff Blooms
Birds and Flowers (Sermon on the Mount)
Jesus in Gethsemane
The Resurrection (garden tomb)

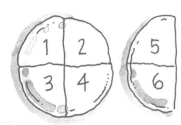

Lemonade

Ingredients
5 medium-sized lemons
5 cups cold water
1 cup sugar

Kitchen Tools
knife for teacher's use
pitcher
measuring cups, spoons
long-handled spoon
paper cups
paper towels

Guide Each Child To
1. Watch as the teacher cuts the lemons so that each child can have part of a lemon.
2. Squeeze his part of the lemon into the pitcher.
3. Help add water and sugar.
4. Take a turn stirring the mixture.

Talk About
- What is your favorite thing to drink?
- How do you know when you need a drink?
- What did the people in our story drink? What happened?

Suggested Bible Stories
Water From a Rock
Ravens Feed Elijah
Daniel Refuses the King's Food
Writing on the Wall
Water Into Wine
The Lord's Supper

Cinnamon Cookies

Ingredients (for about 2 dozen)

¾ cup margarine
¼ cup sugar
1 teaspoon vanilla

1½ cups flour
½ teaspoon cinnamon
¼ cup sugar

Kitchen Tools

large and small mixing bowls
baking sheet
electric mixer
oven
measuring cups, spoons
pot holders

mixing spoon
paper plates
paper towels
sandwich bag
gift wrap ribbon

Prepare Ahead of Time

Beat the margarine, sugar, and vanilla until light and fluffy. Add the flour and beat at low speed until well-blended. Refrigerate for at least 1 hour.

At the beginning of the activity, set the oven at 375 degrees.

Guide Each Child To

1. Help mix cinnamon and sugar in the small bowl and put some on her paper plate.
2. Take a tablespoonful of dough and roll it gently into a ball.
3. Roll the dough in the cinnamon-sugar mixture.
4. Place the dough ball onto an ungreased baking sheet.
5. Repeat the process several times so that she has several cookies.
6. Bake the cookies at 375 degrees for 8 to 10 minutes. Cool.
7. Place her cookies in a plastic sandwich bag. Tie it with a ribbon to make a gift to take to someone.

Talk About
- Who will you give your gift of cookies to?
- Who gave in our story? What did they give? What happened?
- Why does God want us to be cheerful givers?

Suggested Bible Stories

Joseph's Colorful Coat
Samuel's New Coats
David and Jonathan
Queen of Sheba
A Widow Shares With Elijah
Elisha's Room on the Roof
The Wise Men
Perfume on Jesus' Feet
The Widow's Mite

Storm Soup

Ingredients
beef or chicken consommé or bouillon
croutons

Kitchen Tools
pot
hot plate, stove, or microwave
pot holders
stirring spoon
bowls
plastic spoons
paper towels

Guide Each Child To
1. Help pour the soup into the cooking pot.
2. Take a turn stirring as the soup gets warm, but not boiling hot.
3. Pour some of the soup into his bowl.
4. Place several croutons on top of his soup and pretend these are boats.
5. Blow gently on the soup to make waves, then stir it to make a storm. Watch the "boats" toss up and down.
6. Eat the soup and croutons.

Talk About
• Have you ever been in a storm? What happened?
• Who takes care of you during a storm?
• Who was in a storm in our story? What happened?

Suggested Bible Stories
Noah
Jonah
Jesus Stills the Storm
Jesus Walks on Water
Paul's Shipwreck

Index

Stories from Genesis

Creation of Light and Color
Genesis 1
S Flashlight Lantern 8
   Light on the Path 35
   Mixing Colors 65
   Rainbow Crayons 64
   Translucent or Transparent 66
C Candlesticks 112
   Color Cookies 103

Creation of Sky, Sea, and Land
Genesis 1
S Treasure Hunt 33
   Where Do They Go? 32
C Edible Map 119
   Floating Cloud 113

Creation of Plants
Genesis 1
S Cinnamon Potpourri 14
   Dandelion Seeds 13
   Leaves 40
   Roots 39
   Seed Starters 9
C Bloomin' Apple 145
   Flower Cookies 147
   Fruit Harvest Pizza 123

Creation of Sun, Moon, and Stars
Genesis 1
S Boiled Egg 61
   Night Sparkles 48
   Shadow Tracings 10
C Moon Cookies 88
   Sunshine Muffins 115

Creation of Animals
Genesis 1
S Animals Talk and Walk 53
   Earthworms 11
   Grape Jelly Bird Feeder 20
   Insects 21
   Pets 44
   Where Do They Go? 32
C Chocolate Cherry Bird Nests 85
   Corn Cake Lions 91
   Cracker Fish in Soup 108
   English Muffin Animals 79
   Fish Dinner 120

Creation of People
Genesis 1, 2
S Eyes 25
   Hand Friction 12

   Smelling Chart 24
C Breadstick People 131
   Cooperation Cookies 100
   Double Thumbprint Cookies 128
   Honey Crunch Bananas 98
   Tuna Salad 106

Garden of Eden
Genesis 1–3
S Leaves 40
   Roots 39
   Seasonal Smells 59
   Seed Starters 9
C Flower Cookies 147

Adam Names the Animals
Genesis 2
S Pets 44

Adam and Eve Eat the Fruit
Genesis 3
S Natural Laws 50
   Pulling 68
   Sound Waves 54
   Taste the Difference 26
C Bloomin' Apple 145
   Cinnamon Toast 139
   Crunchy Chewies 117
   Fruit Harvest Pizza 123
   Fruit Yogurt Sundaes 144
   Health Muffins 127
   Tuna Salad 106

Adam and Eve Have a Family
Genesis 4
S Measuring 73
C Apple Honey Nutters 86
   Kiss Cookies 83

Noah
Genesis 6–9
S A Good Roof 30
   Animals Talk and Walk 53
   Bubble Rainbow 63
   Building Higher 57
   Earthworms 11
   Erosion 34
   Grape Jelly Bird Feeder 20
   Insects 21
   Mixing Colors 65
   Rainbow Crayons 64
   Seasonal Smells 59
   Sink or Float 69
   Smelling Chart 24
   Sound Waves 54

   Tornado in a Bottle 37
   Volcano 38
   Water Pouring 46
   Weather Wheel 22
   Where Do They Go? 32
   Which Season? 45
   Will It Last? 52
C Cheese Logs 90
   Chocolate Cherry Bird Nests 85
   Color Cookies 103
   Corn Cake Lions 91
   Dyed Eggs 136
   English Muffin Animals 79
   Hot Chocolate Mix 76
   Mini Icees 135
   Peanut Butter 104
   Rainbow Cake 80
   Rainbow Sandwiches 146
   Storm Soup 150

Tower of Babel
Genesis 11
S A Good Roof 30
   Building Higher 57
C Cheese Logs 90
   Pine-Orange Whip 114

Abraham Travels
Genesis 12, 13
S Falling 60
   Pulling 68
   Texture Walk 23
C Crunchy Chewies 117

Abraham and Lot
Genesis 13
S Taste the Difference 26
   Peaceful Water 36
C Biscuit Sheep 95
   Edible Map 119
   Pine-Orange Whip 114

God's Promise to Abraham
Genesis 15
S Flashlight Lantern 8
   Night Sparkles 48
   Sound Waves 54
   Will It Last? 52
C Cinnamon Stars 132

Abraham and the Three Visitors
Genesis 18
S Bubble Rainbow 63
   Seed Matching 42

Index

C Apricot Tea 110
  Chicken Noodle Soup 77
  Fruit Harvest Pizza 123
  Fruit Pies 92
  Fruit Yogurt Sundaes 144
  Giant Cookie 96
  Ham Rolls 84
  Toasty Peanut Sticks 116
  Tuna Salad 106

Isaac Is Born
Genesis 21
S Measuring 73
C Happy Face Cookies 93
  Honey Crunch Bananas 98
  Hot Cider 126

Isaac Gets a Wife
Genesis 24
S Animals Talk and Walk 53
  Cinnamon Potpourri 14
  Oil and Water 58
  Push a Box 71
  Texture Walk 23
C Apple Honey Nutters 86
  English Muffin Animals 79
  Honey Pops 97
  Hot Chocolate Mix 76
  Kiss Cookies 83
  Peach Sherbet 124
  Peanut Butter Delight 109
  Treasure Salad 81

Jacob and Esau
Genesis 25
S Measuring 73
C English Muffin Pizza 111
  Happy Face Cookies 93
  Peanut Butter Delight 109

Birthright and Blessing
Genesis 25, 27
S Pop the Corn 67
  Seasonal Smells 59
  Seed Matching 42
C Apple Cinnamon Muffins 133
  Chicken Noodle Soup 77
  Fruit Harvest Pizza 123
  Honey Crunch Bananas 98
  Tuna Salad 106

Jacob's Dream
Genesis 28
S Balance Beam 56
  Block Bed 51

  Boiled Egg 61
  Falling 60
  Flashlight Lantern 8
  Night Sparkles 48
  Will It Last? 52
C Cinnamon Angels 99
  Cinnamon Stars 132
  Egg Salad Sandwich 102
  Moon Cookies 88
  Pigs in a Blanket 130

Jacob and Rachel
Genesis 29
C Biscuit Sheep 95
  Fruit Pies 92
  Kiss Cookies 83
  Noodle Nibbles 122
  Rapid Rise Rolls 129

Joseph's Colorful Coat
Genesis 37
S Cinnamon Potpourri 14
  Mixing Colors 65
  Rainbow Crayons 64
C Cinnamon Cookies 149
  Color Cookies 103
  Dyed Eggs 136
  Honey Crunch Bananas 98
  Honey Pops 97
  Rainbow Cake 80
  Rainbow Sandwiches 146

Joseph's Dreams
Genesis 27
S Big and Little Clothes 74
  Block Bed 51
  Grain 41
  Night Sparkles 48
C Barley Soup 94
  Cinnamon Stars 132
  Moon Cookies 88
  Pigs in a Blanket 130
  Sunshine Muffins 115

Joseph Is Taken to Egypt
Genesis 37
S Texture Walk 23
C Peanut Butter 104

Joseph in Prison
Genesis 40
S Paper Jail 70
C Crunchy Chewies 117
  Fruit Pies 92

Pharaoh's Dreams
Genesis 41
S Block Bed 51
  Dandelion Seeds 13
  Grain 41
  Liquid Soap 15
C Barley Soup 94
  Pigs in a Blanket 130
  Sweet Potatoes
    With Cinnamon 87

Joseph Leads Egypt
Genesis 41
S Falling 60
  Magnets 62
C Crunchy Chewies 117
  Honey Cookies 125

Joseph's Brothers Go to Egypt
Genesis 42
S Grain 41
  Measuring 73
  Seed Matching 42
C Barley Soup 94
  Ham Rolls 84
  Silver Dollar Pancakes 105

Egypt to the Promised Land
Baby Moses
Exodus 1, 2
S Big and Little Clothes 74
  Liquid Soap 15
  Measuring 73
  Oil and Water 58
C Apple Honey Nutters 86
  Banana Muffins 134
  Berry Bush Pies 141
  Egg Salad Sandwich 102
  Peanut Butter 104
  Rapid Rise Rolls 129

Burning Bush
Exodus 3, 4
S Fire Safety 72
  Hand Friction 12
  Leaves 40
  Roots 39
  Seasonal Smells 59
  Sound Waves 54
C Bloomin' Apple 145
  Cheese Fry Campfires 137

Index

Israelites Work for Pharaoh
Exodus 1, 5
S Building Higher 57

Moses and Aaron Before Pharaoh
Exodus 7
C Noodle Nibbles 122
Rapid Rise Rolls 129

The Plagues in Egypt
Exodus 7–11
S Balance Beam 56
Insects 21
Natural Laws 50
Sound Waves 54
Tornado in a Bottle 37
Water Pouring 46
Weather Wheel 22
C Cinnamon Stars 132
Hot Cider 126
Mini Icees 135

Crossing the Red Sea
Exodus 13, 14
S Air: What You Can't See 16
Feather Pushing 17
Magnets 62
Music Maker 55
Sink or Float 69
Sound Matching 27
Texture Walk 23
Volcano 38
Water Magnifier 47
C Crunchy Chewies 117
Egg Salad Sandwich 102
Floating Cloud 113
Honey Cookies 125

**God Leads Israel With
a Pillar of Fire**
Exodus 13
S Fire Safety 72
Light on the Path 35
Night Sparkles 48
Translucent or Transparent 66
C Candlesticks 112
Cinnamon Stars 132

Manna and Quail
Exodus 16, Numbers 11
S Pop the Corn 67
Seed Matching 42
Will It Last? 52
C Apple Cinnamon Muffins 133
Fruit Harvest Pizza 123

Ham Rolls 84
Honey Crunch Bananas 98
Toasty Peanut Sticks 116
Tuna Salad 106

The Ten Commandments
Exodus 20
S Natural Laws 50
Pulling 68
What's It Made Of? 31
C Cinnamon Toast 139
Crunchy Chewies 117
Health Muffins 127

Building the Tabernacle
Exodus 36
S A Good Roof 30
Building Higher 57

Twelve Spies
Numbers 13, 14
S Natural Laws 50
Taste the Difference 26
C Edible Map 119
Fruit Yogurt Sundaes 144
Fruity Cream Cheese
Sandwiches 78
Gingerbread People 138
Tuna Salad 106

Israelites Wander in the Wilderness
Numbers
S Natural Laws 50
Texture Walk 23
C Edible Map 119
Fruit Pies 92
Hot Cider 126

Aaron's Staff Blooms
Numbers 17
S Leaves 40
Roots 39
C Bloomin' Apple 145
Flower Cookies 147

Water From a Rock
Numbers 20
S Falling 60
Oil and Water 58
Rock Scratching 18
C Lemonade 148

Balaam's Talking Donkey
Numbers 22
S Animals Talk and Walk 53

Pets 44
Where Do They Go? 32
C Crunchy Chewies 117
English Muffin Animals 79

Rahab and the Spies
Joshua 2
C Banana Muffins 134
Berry Bush Pies 141
Noodle Nibbles 122
Peanut Butter 104

Jericho's Walls Fall Down
Joshua 6
S A Good Roof 30
Balance Beam 56
Falling 60
Feather Pushing 17
C Arrow Cheese Toast 82
Hot Cider 126

The Sun Stands Still
Joshua 10
S Boiled Egg 61
Feather Pushing 17
Light on the Path 35
Magnets 62
Shadow Tracings 10
Translucent or Transparent 66
Weather Wheel 22
C Egg Salad Sandwich 102
Honey Cookies 125
Moon Cookies 88
Sunshine Muffins 115

Deborah
Judges 4
S Magnets 62
C Apple Wheel Pancakes 89
Arrow Cheese Toast 82
Honey Cookies 125

Gideon
Judges 6
S Fire Safety 72
Flashlight Lantern 8
Light on the Path 35
Magnets 62
Night Sparkles 48
Translucent or Transparent 66
C Arrow Cheese Toast 82
Candlesticks 112
Cheese Fry Campfires 137
Honey Cookies 125
Moon Cookies 88

Index

Samson
Judges 13–16
S Eyes 25
   Heavy and Light 49
   Magnets 62
C Cinnamon Angels 99
   Corn Cake Lions 91
   Double Thumbprint Cookies 128
   English Muffin Pizza 111
   Gingerbread People 138
   Pigs in a Blanket 130

Ruth
Ruth 1–4
S Dandelion Seeds 13
   Grain 41
   Liquid Soap 15
   Measuring 73
   Pop the Corn 67
   Seed Matching 42
   Seed Starters 9
   Taste the Difference 26
   Texture Walk 23
C Apple Honey Nutters 86
   Apricot Tea 110
   Banana Muffins 134
   Barley Soup 94
   Berry Bush Pies 141
   Chicken Noodle Soup 77
   Cooperation Cookies 100
   Gingerbread People 138
   Ham Rolls 84
   Kiss Cookies 83
   Noodle Nibbles 122
   Rapid Rise Rolls 129
   Sweet Potatoes With
     Cinnamon 87

Hannah Prays for a Baby
1 Samuel 1
S Push a Box 71
   Will It Last? 52
C Happy Face Cookies 93
   Peach Sherbet 124

Samuel's New Coats
1 Samuel 2
S Big and Little Clothes 74
   Cinnamon Potpourri 14
C Cinnamon Cookies 149
   Honey Pops 97

Samuel Hears God
1 Samuel 3
S Big and Little Clothes 74

   Block Bed 51
   Flashlight Lantern 8
   Night Sparkles 48
   Sound Waves 54
   What's It Made Of? 31
C Cinnamon Stars 132
   Hot Cider 126
   Pigs in a Blanket 130

Kings and Prophets

Saul Looks for Lost Donkeys
1 Samuel 9
C English Muffin Animals 79
   Noodle Nibbles 122

David, the Shepherd Boy
1 Samuel 16, Psalms
S Animals Talk and Walk 53
   Big and Little Clothes 74
   Pets 44
C Biscuit Sheep 95
   Corn Cake Lions 91
   Noodle Nibbles 122
   Rapid Rise Rolls 129

David Is Anointed
1 Samuel 16
S Magnets 62
   Oil and Water 58
C Breadstick People 131
   English Muffin Pizza 111
   Honey Cookies 125

David Plays the Harp
1 Samuel 16
S Light to See 43
   Music Maker 55
   Peaceful Water 36
   Push a Box 71
   Sound Matching 27
   Water Magnifier 47
C Biscuit Sheep 95
   Peach Sherbet 124

David and Goliath
1 Samuel 17
S Balance Beam 56
   Big and Little Clothes 74
   Falling 60
   Rock Scratching 18
   Volcano 38
C Egg Salad Sandwich 102
   Peanut Butter 104

David and Jonathan
1 Samuel 18
S Bubble Rainbow 63
   Cinnamon Potpourri 14
C Apricot Tea 110
   Arrow Cheese Toast 82
   Chicken Noodle Soup 77
   Cinnamon Cookies 149
   Cooperation Cookies 100
   Double Thumbprint Cookies 128
   Giant Cookie 96
   Honey Pops 97
   Pine-Orange Whip 114

David Spares Saul's Life at Night
1 Samuel 26
S Flashlight Lantern 8
   Taste the Difference 26
C Cheese Fry Campfires 137

David and Mephibosheth
2 Samuel 2, 9
S Bubble Rainbow 63
C Breadstick People 131
   Chicken Noodle Soup 77
   Gingerbread People 138

Solomon's Dream
1 Kings 3
S Flashlight Lantern 8
   Magnets 62
   Night Sparkles 48
C Cinnamon Stars 132
   Honey Cookies 125
   Pigs in a Blanket 130

Solomon Builds the Temple
1 Kings 6
S A Good Roof 30
   Building Higher 57
   Sound Matching 27
C Apple Wheel Pancakes 89
   Cheese Logs 90
   Sweet Potatoes With
     Cinnamon 87
   Treasure Salad 81

Queen of Sheba
1 Kings 10
S Cinnamon Potpourri 14
   Texture Walk 23
C Cinnamon Cookies 149

Index

Ravens Feed Elijah
1 Kings 17
S Grape Jelly Bird Feeder 20
   Pets 44
   Pop the Corn 67
   Pulling 68
   Seed Matching 42
   Where Do They Go? 32
   Which Season? 45
   Will It Last? 52
C Apple Cinnamon Muffins 133
   Chocolate Cherry Bird Nests 85
   Fruit Harvest Pizza 123
   Ham Rolls 84
   Honey Crunch Bananas 98
   Lemonade 148
   Tuna Salad 106

A Widow Shares With Elijah
1 Kings 17
S Bubble Rainbow 63
   Pop the Corn 67
   Oil and Water 58
   Seed Matching 42
C Apricot Tea 110
   Cinnamon Cookies 149
   Fruit Harvest Pizza 123
   Giant Cookie 96
   Honey Pops 97
   Rapid Rise Rolls 129
   Toasty Peanut Sticks 116
   Tuna Salad 106

Elijah on Mt. Carmel
1 Kings 18
S Feather Pushing 17
   Fire Safety 72
   Push a Box 71
   Rock Scratching 18
   Smelling Chart 24
   Weather Wheel 22
C Cheese Fry Campfires 137
   Cloud Gelatin 143
   Floating Cloud 113
   Honey Cookies 125
   Hot Cider 126

Elijah Goes Up to Heaven
1 Kings 19; 2 Kings 2
S Air: What You Can't See 16
   Feather Pushing 17
C Apple Wheel Pancakes 89
   Cooperation Cookies 100
   Heavenly Fruit Snack 101

A Widow's Oil Jars
2 Kings 4
S Measuring 73
   Oil and Water 58
   What's It Made Of? 31
C Banana Muffins 134
   Berry Bush Pies 141
   Noodle Nibbles 122
   Pine Orange Whip 114
   Rapid Rise Rolls 129

Elisha's Room on the Roof
2 Kings 4
S A Good Roof 30
   Bubble Rainbow 63
   Building Higher 57
   Flashlight Lantern 8
C Apricot Tea 110
   Cheese Logs 90
   Chicken Noodle Soup 77
   Cinnamon Cookies 149
   Giant Cookie 96
   Honey Crunch Bananas 98
   Peanut Butter Delight 109

Naaman
2 Kings 5
S Balance Beam 56
   Big and Little Clothes 74
   Liquid Soap 15
   My Body 29
   What's It Made Of? 31
C Cinnamon Toast 139
   Crunchy Chewies 117
   Dyed Eggs 136
   Gingerbread People 138
   Health Muffins 127

An Ax Head Floats
2 Kings 6
C Berry Bush Pies 141
   Noodle Nibbles 122
   Rapid Rise Rolls 129

Servant Sees God's Army
2 Kings 6
S Falling 60
   Rock Salt 19
   Volcano 38
C Apple Wheel Pancakes 89
   Arrow Cheese Toast 82

Singers Lead Jehoshaphat's Army
2 Chronicles 20
S Magnets 62

   Music Maker 55
   Push a Box 71
   Sound Matching 27
   Water Magnifier 47
   Which Season? 45
C Arrow Cheese Toast 82
   Honey Cookies 125

King Hezekiah Gets Well
2 Kings 20
S My Body 29
   Shadow Tracings 10

King Josiah Finds God's Word
2 Kings 22, 23
S Natural Laws 50
   Pulling 68
C Cinnamon Toast 139
   Crunchy Chewies 117
   Health Muffins 127
   Scroll Rolls 140
   Treasure Cookies 118

Rebuilding Jerusalem's Walls
Nehemiah 2–6
S A Good Roof 30
   Building Higher 57
   Light to See 43
   Sound Matching 27
   Texture Walk 23
C Banana Muffins 134
   Cheese Logs 90
   Honey Cookies 125
   Pine-Orange Whip 114

Esther
Esther 1–10
S Magnets 62
   Seasonal Smells 59
   Taste the Difference 26
C Egg Salad Sandwich 102
   Fruit Punch 142
   Ham Rolls 84
   Honey Cookies 125
   Kiss Cookies 83
   Treasure Salad 81

Daniel Refuses the King's Food
Daniel 1
S Pop the Corn 67
   Pulling 68
   Seasonal Smells 59
   Seed Matching 42
   Smelling Chart 24
   What's It Made Of? 31

C Apple Cinnamon Muffins 133
  Cooperation Cookies 100
  Fruit Harvest Pizza 123
  Ham Rolls 84
  Lemonade 148
  Pine-Orange Whip 114
  Tuna Salad 106

The Fiery Furnace
Daniel 3
S Balance Beam 56
  Falling 60
  Fire Safety 72
  Seasonal Smells 59
  Taste the Difference 26
  Volcano 38
C Cheese Fry Campfires 137
  Cooperation Cookies 100
  Double Thumbprint Cookies 128
  Egg Salad Sandwich 102
  Peanut Butter 104

Writing on the Wall
Daniel 5
S Balance Beam 56
  Hand Friction 12
C Fruit Punch 142
  Lemonade 148

Daniel and the Lions
Daniel 6
S Animals Talk and Walk 53
  Feather Pushing 17
  Night Sparkles 48
  Pets 44
  Taste the Difference 26
  Volcano 38
  Where Do They Go? 32
  Which Season? 45
C Cinnamon Angels 99
  Corn Cake Lions 91
  Egg Salad Sandwich 102
  Peach Sherbet 124
  Peanut Butter 104
  Pigs in a Blanket 130

Jonah
Jonah 1–4
S Dandelion Seeds 13
  Natural Laws 50
  Pulling 68
  Shadow Tracings 10
  Sink or Float 69
  Smelling Chart 24
  Taste the Difference 26

  Tornado in a Bottle 37
  Water Pouring 46
  Weather Wheel 22
  What's It Made Of? 31
C Cinnamon Toast 139
  Cracker Fish in Soup 108
  English Muffin Animals 79
  Fish Dinner 120
  Health Muffins 127
  Hot Cider 126
  Mini Icees 135
  Peanut Butter 104
  Rainbow Cake 80
  Storm Soup 150

Jesus' Life, Death, and Resurrection
Gabriel Appears to Mary
Luke 1
S Sound Waves 54
C Cinnamon Angels 99

John the Baptist Is Born
Luke 1
S Face Sculpture 28
  Sound Waves 54
C Cinnamon Angels 99
  Hot Cider 126

Jesus Is Born
Luke 2
S Animals Talk and Walk 53
  Flashlight Lantern 8
  Pets 44
C Mangers 121
  Sunshine Muffins 115

Angels Appear to the Shepherds
Luke 2
S Peaceful Water 36
  Sound Matching 27
  Water Magnifier 47
C Biscuit Sheep 95
  Cinnamon Angels 99
  Cinnamon Stars 132

The Wise Men
Matthew 2
S Cinnamon Potpourri 14
  Night Sparkles 48
  Smelling Chart 24
  Texture Walk 23
C Cinnamon Cookies 149
  Cinnamon Stars 132

  Honey Pops 97
  Peanut Butter Delight 109
  Pigs in a Blanket 130

Anna and Simeon
Luke 2
S Sound Matching 27
  Water Magnifier 47
C Fruit Pies 92
  Hot Cider 126

Joseph, Mary, and Jesus Go to Egypt
Matthew 2
S Block Bed 51
  Texture Walk 23
C Egg Salad Sandwich 102

Jesus as a Boy in the Temple
Luke 2
S Big and Little Clothes 74
C Scroll Rolls 140

John the Baptist
Matthew 3
S Insects 21
  Magnets 62
  Oil and Water 58
  Pop the Corn 67
  Water Pouring 46
C Apple Cinnamon Muffins 133
  Breadstick People 131
  English Muffin Pizza 111
  Fruit Yogurt Sundaes 144
  Gingerbread People 138
  Tuna Salad 106

Jesus Is Baptized
Matthew 3
S Grape Jelly Bird Feeder 20
  Oil and Water 58
  Water Pouring 46
  Which Season? 45
C Chocolate Cherry Bird Nests 85
  Dyed Eggs 136

Jesus Is Tempted
Matthew 4
S Rock Scratching 18
  Taste the Difference 26
C Cinnamon Toast 139
  Health Muffins 127

Index

Jesus Chooses Twelve Friends
Matthew 4; Mark 2, 3
S Earthworms 11
 Magnets 62
C Banana Muffins 134
 Cooperation Cookies 100
 Cracker Fish in Soup 108
 Double Thumbprint Cookies 128
 Fish Dinner 120
 Gingerbread People 138
 Noodle Nibbles 122
 Pine-Orange Whip 114
 Rapid Rise Rolls 129

The Transfiguration
Matthew 17
S Which Season? 45

The Triumphal Entry
Mark 11
S Animals Talk and Walk 53
 Dandelion Seeds 13
 Music Maker 55
 Pets 44
 Roots 39
 Sound Matching 27
 Texture Walk 23
 Water Magnifier 47
C Bloomin' Apple 145

Jesus Washes His Friends' Feet
John 13
S Magnets 62
 Oil and Water 58
 Will It Last? 52
C Banana Muffins 134
 Berry Bush Pies 141
 Noodle Nibbles 122

The Lord's Supper
Matthew 26
S Light to See 43
 Pop the Corn 67
 Seed Matching 42
 Smelling Chart 24
C Apple Cinnamon Muffins 133
 Fruit Harvest Pizza 123
 Fruit Yogurt Sundaes 144
 Lemonade 148
 Toasty Peanut Sticks 116

Jesus in Gethsemane
Matthew 26
S Leaves 40
 Roots 39

C Cheese Fry Campfires 137
 Flower Cookies 147

The Resurrection
Luke 24
S Balance Beam 56
 Feather Pushing 17
 Leaves 40
 Rock Scratching 18
 Roots 39
 Volcano 38
 Water Magnifier 47
 Will It Last? 52
C Bloomin' Apple 145
 Cinnamon Angels 99
 Flower Cookies 147
 Hot Cider 126

Road to Emmaus
Luke 24
S Light to See 43

Jesus Makes Breakfast for His Friends
John 21
S Earthworms 11
 Pop the Corn 67
 Seasonal Smells 59
 Seed Matching 42
 Smelling Chart 24
C Apple Honey Nutters 86
 Cheese Fry Campfires 137
 Chicken Noodle Soup 77
 Cracker Fish in Soup 108
 English Muffin Animals 79
 Fish Dinner 120
 Fruit Harvest Pizza 123

Jesus Goes Back to Heaven
Acts 1
C Cinnamon Angels 99
 Cloud Gelatin 143
 Floating Cloud 113
 Heavenly Fruit Snack 101

Jesus' Miracles
Water Into Wine
John 2
S Balance Beam 56
 Oil and Water 58
C Fruit Punch 142
 Lemonade 148

The Great Catch of Fish
Luke 5
S Earthworms 11
 Pulling 6
 Seasonal Smells 59
 Smelling Chart 24
 What's It Made Of? 31
 Where Do They Go? 32
C Cracker Fish in Soup 108
 English Muffin Animals 79
 Fish Dinner 120

Peter's Mother-in-Law
Matthew 8
S Measuring 73
 My Body 29

Through the Roof
Luke 5
S Heavy and Light 49
 My Body 29
C Breadstick People 131
 Cooperation Cookies 100
 Gingerbread People 138
 Noodle Nibbles 122
 Pine-Orange Whip 114
 Rapid Rise Rolls 129

Lame Man at the Pool
John 5
S Feather Pushing 17
 Water Pouring 46

The Centurion's Sick Servant
Matthew 8
S My Body 29

The Man's Withered Hand
Matthew 12
S Hand Friction 12
 My Body 29
C Breadstick People 131

Jesus Stills the Storm
Mark 4
S Air: What You Can't See 16
 Erosion 34
 Peaceful Water 36
 Sink or Float 69
 Tornado in a Bottle 37
 Volcano 38
 Water Pouring 46
 Weather Wheel 22
 Which Season? 45

C Mini Icees 135
  Pigs in a Blanket 130
  Rainbow Cake 80
  Storm Soup 150

Woman Touches Jesus' Hem
Luke 8
S Falling 60
  My Body 29
C Breadstick People 131

Jairus's Daughter
Luke 8
S Balance Beam 56
  Big and Little Clothes 74
  Feather Pushing 17
  Measuring 73
  My Body 29

Jesus Feeds 5,000
Luke 9
S Big and Little Clothes 74
  Bubble Rainbow 63
  Light to See 43
  Pop the Corn 67
  Seasonal Smells 59
  Seed Matching 42
  Smelling Chart 24
C Apricot Tea 110
  Chicken Noodle Soup 77
  Cracker Fish in Soup 108
  Fish Dinner 120
  Fruit Harvest Pizza 123
  Giant Cookie 96
  Ham Rolls 84
  Honey Crunch Bananas 98
  Honey Pops 97
  Sweet Potatoes With
    Cinnamon 87
  Toasty Peanut Sticks 116
  Tuna Salad 106

Jesus Walks on Water
Matthew 14
S Air: What You Can't See 16
  Balance Beam 56
  Sink or Float 69
  Texture Walk 23
  Tornado in a Bottle 37
  Volcano 38
  Water Pouring 46
  Weather Wheel 22
C Storm Soup 150

Tax Money in a Fish
Matthew 17
S Animals Talk and Walk 53
  Earthworms 11
  Pets 44
  Seasonal Smells 59
  Where Do They Go? 32
C Cracker Fish in Soup 108
  English Muffin Animals 79
  Fish Dinner 120
  Honey Crunch Bananas 98
  Silver Dollar Pancakes 105
  Treasure Cookies 118

Jesus Heals a Blind Man With Mud
John 9
S Eyes 25
  Face Sculpture 28
  Light on the Path 35
  Rock Salt 19
C Peanut Butter Delight 109

Jesus Heals the Bent Woman
Luke 13
S My Body 29
C Breadstick People 131
  Gingerbread People 138

Ten Lepers
Luke 17
S Light to See 43
  My Body 29
C Breadstick People 131
  Gingerbread People 138
  Sweet Potatoes With
    Cinnamon 87

Blind Bartimaeus
Mark 10
S Eyes 25
  Face Sculpture 28
  Falling 60
  Light on the Path 35
  Rock Salt 19
C Breadstick People 131
  Peanut Butter Delight 109

Lazarus
John 11
S Feather Pushing 17
  Light to See 43
  My Body 29

Jesus' Teachings
Nicodemus Visits Jesus at Night
John 3
S Night Sparkles 48
  Sound Waves 54
C Cheese Fry Campfires 137
  Cinnamon Stars 132
  Moon Cookies 88

The Woman at the Well
John 4
S Oil and Water 58
  Water Pouring 46

The Beatitudes
Matthew 5
S Peaceful Water 36

Let Your Light Shine
Matthew 5
S Boiled Egg 61
  Light on the Path 35
  Water Magnifier 47
C Candlesticks 112

Birds and Flowers
Matthew 6
S Dandelion Seeds 13
  Grape Jelly Bird Feeder 20
  Leaves 40
  Mixing Colors 65
  Pets 44
  Rainbow Crayons 64
  Roots 39
  Seasonal Smells 59
  Where Do They Go? 32
C Bloomin' Apple 145
  Chocolate Cherry Bird Nests 85
  Flower Cookies 147
  Tuna Salad 106

The Lord's Prayer
Matthew 6
S Push a Box 71
C Heavenly Fruit Snack 101
  Peach Sherbet 124
  Toasty Peanut Sticks 116

The Wise Man's House
Matthew 7
S A Good Roof 30
  Building Higher 57
  Erosion 34
  Natural Laws 50
  Water Pouring 46

Index

C Cinnamon Toast 139
  Crunchy Chewies 117
  Health Muffins 127
  Heavenly Fruit Snack 101

The Sower and the Seeds
Luke 8
S Dandelion Seeds 13
  Seed Starters 9

The Pearl of Great Price
Matthew 13
C Silver Dollar Pancakes 105

Hidden Treasure
Matthew 13
S Treasure Hunt 33
C Silver Dollar Pancakes 105
  Treasure Cookies 118
  Treasure Salad 81

The Fish and the Net
Matthew 13
C Cracker Fish in Soup 108
  Fish Dinner 120

The Good Samaritan
Luke 10
S Pets 44
  Texture Walk 23
C Apple Honey Nutters 86
  Banana Muffins 134
  Berry Bush Pies 141
  Pine-Orange Whip 114

Bigger Barns
Luke 12
S A Good Roof 30
  Building Higher 57
  Grain 41
C Barley Soup 94

The Wheat and the Weeds
Matthew 13
S Grain 41
  Seed Starters 9
C Barley Soup 94

Mary and Martha
Luke 10
S Liquid Soap 15
  Sound Waves 54
  Taste the Difference 26
C Apple Honey Nutters 86
  Apricot Tea 110

Banana Muffins 134
Fruit Harvest Pizza 123
Noodle Nibbles 122
Tuna Salad 106

The Lost Sheep
Luke 15
S Animals Talk and Walk 53
  Pets 44
  Will It Last? 52
C Biscuit Sheep 95
  Happy Face Cookies 93
  Peanut Butter 104

The Lost Coin
Luke 15
S Will It Last? 52
C Candlesticks 112
  Happy Face Cookies 93
  Silver Dollar Pancakes 105
  Treasure Cookies 118

The Runaway Son
Luke 15
S Measuring 73
  Will It Last? 52
C Fruit Punch 142
  Happy Face Cookies 93

A Pharisee and a Tax Collector Pray
Luke 18
S Push a Box 71
C Peach Sherbet 124

Jesus and the Children
Luke 18
S Big and Little Clothes 74
  Will It Last? 52
C Breadstick People 131
  Double Thumbprint Cookies 128
  English Muffin Pizza 111
  Honey Crunch Bananas 98

Zacchaeus
Luke 19
S Taste the Difference 26
C Breadstick People 131
  English Muffin Pizza 111
  Gingerbread People 138

Perfume on Jesus' Feet
John 12
S Bubble Rainbow 63
  Smelling Chart 24
C Cinnamon Cookies 149

Honey Crunch Bananas 98
Honey Pops 97
Peanut Butter Delight 109

Two Sons and a Vineyard
Matthew 21
S Measuring 73
  Natural Laws 50
  Pulling 68
  What's It Made Of? 31
C Cinnamon Toast 139
  Crunchy Chewies 117
  Fruity Cream Cheese
    Sandwiches 78
  Health Muffins 127

The Widow's Mite
Mark 12
S Cinnamon Potpourri 14
C Cinnamon Cookies 149
  Honey Pops 97
  Silver Dollar Pancakes 105

The Church
Peter and John Heal a Lame Man
Acts 3
S My Body 29
  Sound Matching 27
  Water Magnifier 47
C Breadstick People 131

Philip and the Man From Ethiopia
Acts 8
S Magnets 62
  Oil and Water 58
  Sound Waves 54
  Texture Walk 23
  Water Pouring 46
C Apple Wheel Pancakes 89
  Dyed Eggs 136
  Rapid Rise Rolls 129
  Scroll Rolls 140

Paul to Damascus
Acts 9
S Boiled Egg 61
  Eyes 25
  Face Sculpture 28
  Flashlight Lantern 8
  Light on the Path 35
  Rock Salt 19
  Translucent or Transparent 66
C Peanut Butter Delight 109

Paul in a Basket
Acts 9; 2 Corinthians 11
S Night Sparkles 48
C Banana Muffins 134
  Cinnamon Stars 132
  Cooperation Cookies 100
  Peanut Butter 104

Dorcas
Acts 9
S Liquid Soap 15
  My Body 29
C Apple Honey Nutters 86
  Banana Muffins 134
  Honey Crunch Bananas 98
  Rapid Rise Rolls 129

Peter and Cornelius
Acts 10
S Oil and Water 58
  Water Pouring 46
C Breadstick People 131
  Dyed Eggs 136
  Pigs in a Blanket 130

Peter Escapes From Prison
Acts 12
S Balance Beam 56
  Falling 60
  Flashlight Lantern 8
  Heavy and Light 49
  Night Sparkles 48
  Paper Jail 70
  Push a Box 71
  Which Season? 45
C Cinnamon Angels 99
  Cinnamon Stars 132
  Egg Salad Sandwich 102
  Hot Cider 126
  Pigs in a Blanket 130

Timothy
Acts 16; Philippians 2;
1 Thessalonians 3; 2 Timothy 1
C Pine-Orange Whip 114

Lydia
Acts 16
S Oil and Water 58
  Water Pouring 46
C Chicken Noodle Soup 77
  Dyed Eggs 136

Paul and Silas in Prison
Acts 16
S Balance Beam 56
  Feather Pushing 17
  Music Maker 55
  Night Sparkles 48
  Oil and Water 58
  Paper Jail 70
  Push a Box 71
  Sound Matching 27
  Volcano 38
  Which Season? 45
C Cooperation Cookies 100
  Dyed Eggs 136
  Egg Salad Sandwich 102
  Peach Sherbet 124
  Pine-Orange Whip 114

Paul's Nephew Hears a Plot
Acts 23
S Big and Little Clothes 74
  Night Sparkles 48
  Paper Jail 70
C Cinnamon Stars 132
  Peanut Butter 104

Paul's Shipwreck
Acts 27
S Air: What You Can't See 16
  Erosion 34
  Falling 60
  Sink or Float 69
  Tornado in a Bottle 37
  Volcano 38
  Weather Wheel 22
C Edible Map 119
  Egg Salad Sandwich 102
  Ham Rolls 84
  Mini Icees 135
  Peanut Butter 104
  Storm Soup 150

Paul on Malta
Acts 28
S Fire Safety 72
  Which Season? 45
C Cheese Fry Campfires 137

John Sees Heaven
Revelation 21
S Boiled Egg 61
  Light on the Path 35
  Mixing Colors 65
  Rainbow Crayons 64
  Sound Matching 27
  Translucent or Transparent 66
C Candlesticks 112
  Cinnamon Angels 99
  Cloud Gelatin 143
  Color Cookies 103
  Heavenly Fruit Snack 101
  Rainbow Cake 80
  Sunshine Muffins 115